More Critical acclaim for *Value Based Management:*

"Jim Knight is right on! To maximize shareholder value, business processes must be aligned from the CEO down to the shop floor. Everyone on the team has to be focused, measured, and incented to pull in the same direction."

—*Lou Rupnik*
Senior Vice President of Business Development
Xerox

"Jim Knight convincingly tells why corporate governance ought to be focused on shareholder value; more importantly, he reveals how those responsible for setting the corporate direction can infuse value maximization considerations into all of their decision making activities."

—*Dennis E. Logue*
Steven Roth Professor of Management
The Amos Tuck School, Dartmouth College

"James Knight's new book is a thoughtful, step-by-step analysis and implementation guide, emphasizing the critical factors any company can follow to achieve improved value based management."

—*Richard Ferry*
Chairman
Korn/Ferry International

VALUE BASED MANAGEMENT

VALUE BASED MANAGEMENT

Developing a Systematic
Approach to Creating
Shareholder Value

JAMES A. KNIGHT

McGraw-Hill

New York • San Francisco • Washington, D.C. • Auckland
Bogotá • Caracas • Lisbon • London • Madrid • Mexico City
Milan • Montreal • New Delhi • San Juan • Singapore
Sydney • Tokyo • Toronto

Library of Congress Cataloging-in-Publication Data

Knight, James A. (James Atwood), date.
  Value-based management: developing a systematic approach to creating
shareholder value/James A. Knight.
    p. cm.
  ISBN 0-7863-1133-9
  1. Value analysis (Cost control) 2. Industrial management.
I. Title.
HD47.3.K595 1997
658.15'52—dc21   97-8662
                                                            CIP

McGraw-Hill

A Division of The McGraw·Hill Companies

    5 6 7 8 9 0   FGR/FGR   0 2 1 0

IBSN 0-7863-1133-9

The sponsoring editor for this book was Steven Sheehan, the editing
supervisor was Donna Namorato, and the production supervisor was Suzanne
W. B. Rapcavage. It was set in Palatino by Bi-Comp, Inc.

Printed and bound by Quebecor/Fairfield.

This publication is designed to provide accurate and authoritative information
in regard to the subject matter covered. It is sold with the understanding that
neither the author nor the publisher is engaged in rendering legal, accounting,
or other professional service. If legal advice or other expert assistance is
required, the services of a competent professional person should be sought.

> *—From a Declaration of Principles jointly adopted by a Committee*
> *of the American Bar Association and a Committee of Publishers.*

McGraw-Hill books are available at special quantity discounts to use as
premiums and sales promotions, or for use in corporate training programs. For
more information, please write to the Director of Special Sales, McGraw-Hill,
11 West 19th Street, New York, N.Y. 10011. Or contact your local bookstore.

 This book is printed on recycled, acid-free paper containing a
minimum of 50 percent recycled de-inked fiber.

Hilary, James, Remington, and William
May you have a strong foundation and
stay forever young

C O N T E N T S

ix

Chapter 10

Why Value Management Fails   281

Chapter 11

Summary   295

Let me begin by emphatically stating that this book discusses the creation and implementation of a managerial mind-set focused on value creation. This book is not intended to provide theoretical constructs or mathematical derivations of the many available financial measures that capture aspects of operating performance, shareholder returns, and economic profit. In that sense, this book offers an unusual approach to the topic of value-based management. My goal is to provide a back-to-basics approach by outlining key concepts and providing examples, explanations, diagrams, and case histories demonstrating how every decision a management team makes can consistently create shareholder value.

Value-based management represents more than an accounting treatment of the financial results of operations and capital management. Value-based management instills a mind-set where everyone in the organization learns to prioritize decisions based on their understanding of how those decisions contribute to corporate value. True value-based management creates management alignment by linking the often disparate corporate activities of strategic planning, financial reporting, and compensation/incentive planning. Value-based management succeeds when decision making becomes focused and achieves alignment between strategy, performance measurement, and behavior.

All too often, key concepts of shareholder value become implemented as another budgetary device and then fail to provide the desired results of improved performance. Why does this occur? Because increases in shareholder value cannot be achieved solely with accounting or budgetary magic. Achieving long-term sustained growth in shareholder returns requires basic problem solving and decision making throughout an organization that is aware of the impact of each decision on value creation. It is a mind-set that succeeds by improving stakeholder communication, creatively expanding management's understanding of business alternatives and trade-offs, and sharpening management's ability to set goals and targets.

This book is intended for a broad audience of senior managers, corporate finance personnel, and operating managers. It is intended to provide a frame of reference. Numerous other books are available to explain the accounting or financial calculations. Such books are not required for a basic understanding of value management because for value management to succeed, everyone in the organization should have a straightforward intuitive grasp of how their decision making will affect value creation and impact the organization.

The chapters are organized into four key groups:

1. The first group includes a wide-ranging discussion of the concepts underlying the definition of value. Chapters 1–4 define value creation, explain why management should focus on value, and explain how investor expectations can be achieved.

2. The second group introduces the definitions and concepts underlying value-based decision making. Chapters 5–6 define value management, describe the ingredients necessary to achieve a value-managed organization, outline value-based decision making, and explain the relationship of value-based decision making to strategy execution.

3. The third group outlines key issues involved with implementing value management and value-based decision making. Chapters 7–9 encompass performance measurement selection and alignment, compensation/incentive strategies,

and implementation factors necessary for value-based management to succeed.

4. The fourth group rounds out the discussion of value-based management by identifying the key lessons and ideas critical to its success. Chapters 10–11 outline the key lessons that are learned from some notable examples of implementation failures and summarize the key concepts critical for a successful implementation of value-based management.

Many people contributed to the writing of this book, to whom I am most grateful. I would like to acknowledge their contributions and express my thanks for their efforts on behalf of the book.

Many people over the years have contributed to the ideas in this book, and I thank each of them for their ideas, insights, advice, and wisdom. My thanks to each person for his or her contribution. Any errors in the text that resulted from my misinterpetation or poor expression of ideas are mine alone. Among the many people who helped, a few deserve special thanks.

The people at Times Mirror and McGraw-Hill who believed in the idea for this book, including Mike Junior, Amy Hollands Gaber, and Jim Keefe, who stood by this project and supported it at Irwin for six long years; and Stender Sweeney, who kept the desire burning to get the project done.

The finance and value ideas in this book are the compilation of many years of thoughtful guidance from a number of people. I owe special thanks to Curt Hessler for lighting my fire on value and performance measures a number of years ago; my debating partners at The Boston Consulting Group, including but not limited to Eric Olsen, Rawley Thomas, Ron Nicol, Bob Griswold, Ted Scalise, Neil Monnery, and Henry Elkington; Jim Matheson and Robin Arnold of Strategic Decisions Group; Jim Smith of the University of North Carolina; and Gil Babcock at the University of Southern California.

Clients have contributed immensely to the ideas and practical concepts in the book. Don Macleod, Rick Crowley, Dave Dahmen, and Jim Chamberlain are a few who deserve special mention for their patience over the years. Special thanks as well to the case teams at BCG and SCA who helped me crystallize my thinking.

Assembling the manuscript was a labor of love, and I have Dulcevita Edrozo to thank for hours more numerous than I care to remember fixing the text and turning it around to me in record time. John Kolozak spent many late nights on exhibits. Gina Lee and Victor Yuan contributed many hours of research to support the ideas. David Bart stepped in and provided excellent editorial counseling to complete the manuscript.

My colleagues at SCA were very supportive, especially over the last six months of the project. Lori Siegel and Dan Marcus were constant sources of counsel and support, as were my other partners.

Reviewers provided invaluable feedback, and special thanks go to Joanne Walden, Dave Dahmen, and Dick Bower, who invested selflessly of their time to try and straighten out my fuzzy thinking.

The most precious contribution of all came from my wife, Cynthia, and my children, who gave me the time to write this book.

CHAPTER 1

Managing for Value
Makes a Difference

Today's managers are receiving conflicting signals, signals that prevent the company from achieving its full potential. Management receives these conflicting signals from the performance measures used in each of the management processes, including strategic planning, budgeting, reporting, and compensation. The signals come in the form of planning goals, budget targets, monthly and quarterly financial results, and incentive targets. These signals conflict with one another because the management processes are not aligned. Strategic planning emphasizes one goal or objective, while the budgeting process emphasizes another, and the incentive system rewards a third. A common conflict is a strategic planning process that emphasizes growth, while the annual budget is focused on earnings per share. Is it any wonder managers are confused?

Managers are also confused by differing priorities. This month, a company may be focused on a quality initiative, next month on capabilities enhancement, and the next month on process reengineering. Is it any surprise that managers are skeptical about new initiatives and don't understand how to prioritize them?

There is a solution to the problems created by these conflicting signals and confusing priorities: Adopt the mind-set of managing for value. Managing for value addresses these conflicts by prioritizing each of the initiatives in the context of the company's goal: consistently creating shareholder value. In a value-managed company, the mind-set is reflected in the way decisions are made, the use of resources, and the rewards managers earn.

But the mind-set of managing for value is not enough in and of itself. To achieve maximum value, you must translate the mind-set into reality, using it in frontline decision making in the daily operating and investment decisions managers are making. Managing for value does not mean just installing a new performance measure such as economic value added. Economic value added is not really a new concept. Alfred Marshall first described it in his 1890 publication of *Principles of Economics*. Economic value added simply means thinking through how you will create value. Managing for value begins with strategy and ends with financial results. If you try to manage financial results without strategy, you will fall short of managing for value. Conversely, if you manage for strategy and fail to deliver financial results, you will fail to create value. Value management is the link between strategy and financial results.

Successful value management requires that a mind-set of managing for value be integrated into the way decisions are made. This approach to decision making begins with the goal—managing for value—and uses measures of financial and nonfinancial performance to support that goal. Measures of performance must be an integral part of both the key management processes (strategic planning, budgeting, reporting, and incentive compensation) and the decisions made to improve operations or make new investments.

Making value management a reality in a company requires management to agree that value maximization is the company's goal. Management must then develop a business strategy to achieve the goal of maximizing value creation. Then management must translate the goal and business strategy into a mind-set in the company that focuses decision making on creating value. The mind-set needs to be included in the way the company measures itself, the processes the company uses for managing itself, and the resource decisions the company makes to improve operations or make new investments.

We can logically divide the topic of value management into five categories: goal, strategy, measures, processes, and decisions. Figure 1–1 illustrates how each of these five categories follows from the one before. A goal requires a strategy

F I G U R E   1–1

Shareholder Value Can Be Created or
Destroyed through Each Level of Company
Decision Making

to achieve the goal. Measures capture the strategy's progress and are used in the management processes to signal good decisions.

CLARIFYING GOALS

In a company managing for value, the company's goal is to deliver value to investors. This does not imply that the company is managed for value to the detriment or exclusion of the customer, the employees, or other important constituents. In fact, as you will see in later chapters, the reverse is true. Managing a company for value requires delivering maximum return to the investors while balancing the interests of the other important constituents, including customers and employees. Companies that consistently deliver value for investors have learned this lesson.

All too often, the company gets confused by multiple objectives. Companies get seduced into believing that no single objective will cover the interests of all the constituents, and the company needs multiple objectives beyond value creation to satisfy the investors. This is a trap that leads to conflicting signals, confusing priorities, and poor decision making. In the end, there can be only one goal for a company owned by shareholders: maximizing value.[1]

Establishing clarity around the objective is the first and most essential step for senior management to complete. Without this clarity, any value management initiative will fall short of expectations and fail to deliver the desired results.

STRATEGY

Strategy is probably the most overused word in business language. Every business person talks about strategy, but the word is used to mean many different things, including objective, vision, what the company does, and how the company competes. These conflicting definitions are confusing and frustrating to many people who are trying to understand a company's strategy. Strategy is also used as an adjective—strategic—to describe a variety of activities, including alliances, partners, initiatives, products, projects, and investments.

Because of this confusion, it is helpful to pause for a moment and define strategy, what a good strategy is, and how good strategy is developed.

Strategy is often confused with a goal or objective. The objective is what you are going to do. The strategy, on the other hand, is how you are going to achieve the objective. Goals and objectives lead to strategy, which leads to the tactics necessary to execute the strategy.

Strategy is also confused with planning. Planning is not strategy. Planning is an expression of how the company will implement its strategy. A plan expresses how the strategy will be executed.

For example, in World War II, the allied objective in Europe was to defeat the German forces. How the allies accomplished their goal was their strategy—that is, drive the German army out of Western Europe.

One reason objectives and strategies are often confused is that the execution of the strategy becomes an objective that generates further specific strategies. In the World War II example, to accomplish the strategy of driving the German army out of Western Europe, the allies had to formulate tactics (more specific strategies) including battle plans, troop deployments, and air sorties. They started with the objective, developed strategies to accomplish the strategy, and formulated tactics that made the strategy actionable.

When applied to a business setting, the objective of a company is to create value (or wealth if you prefer) for the shareholders. The company's strategy-development effort answers the question, "How will the company achieve its objective?" Strategy defines the company's targeted markets and customers by answering the question, "How will the company differentiate itself?" A company can try to achieve the objective in a variety of ways, which is what leads to companies having different strategies.

With the right strategy in place, the company is faced with the challenge of implementing the strategy and measuring progress to achieve the strategy.

PERFORMANCE MEASURES

The performance measures a company chooses need to support and reinforce the company's strategy and help managers achieve the goal of value creation. The performance measures should do more than reflect financial results that only capture events after the fact. Instead, they should help management make good decisions. Performance measures need to reflect the company's business strategy and focus managers on decision making that creates value. Performance measures do not need to reflect financial results. In many cases, it is desirable to balance financial measures with nonfinancial measures, such as customer satisfaction and retention. These types of performance measures address the valid concern of management that the right decisions for business do not always show up in a single period's financial results. Also, the performance measures chosen should be customized for the company, not "off-the-shelf" measures. For example, economic value added is a financial performance measure that has far greater value when it is customized for a specific company. This is true of financial measures and strategic measures as well.

Performance measures do not replace strategy; they capture the results of the strategy. If you have chosen well, the performance measure will capture both the long- and short-term results of the strategy. Performance measures are not a replacement for management judgment. They will do little if anything to improve management decision making. To affect the decision making, you must integrate the performance measures into the management processes.

MANAGEMENT PROCESSES

There are four key management processes to consider when installing value management into any company: strategic planning, budgeting, reporting, and incentives. These management processes need to send consistent signals to managers and reinforce the value mind-set. Performance measures must be included in the processes, and the processes must be designed to reinforce consistent signaling to managers that support the company's strategy. One management process is often focused on one priority, while another is focused on a different priority. The management processes need to be aligned to send consistent signals to managers.

Figure 1–2 illustrates the different management processes and how alignment is required to send a consistent reinforced signal to managers ensuring that they receive the same message from all processes. This consistency is important if you want management to focus on making value-creating decisions.

OPERATING AND INVESTMENT DECISIONS

Value is created in a company through the operating and investment decisions the company makes. Making strategy and value creation actionable within the company means focusing management on making decisions that create value. Daily decision making is what controls the allocation of physical and human resources. By making these operating decisions wisely, managers can create value for investors. Value management becomes a reality when the value management mind-set is embedded in the operating and investment decisions the company is making. Getting

8   CHAPTER 1

FIGURE 1–2

To Successfully Manage Value, the Processes Must
Be Consistent

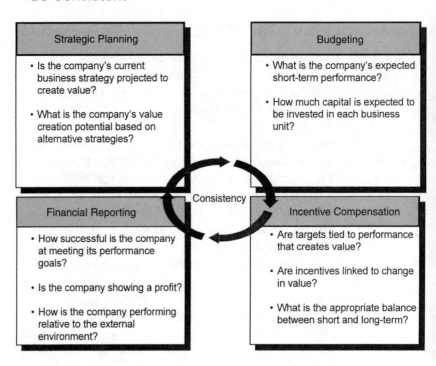

managers to think about and focus on value will improve
the company's performance.

EXAMPLE: ACME ELECTRONICS

An example of the link between strategy and financial results is a company we will call Acme. Acme is a real company whose name and results are disguised. Acme was a
laggard performer in its industry until it adopted a mind-
set of managing for value. After becoming a value-managed
company, Acme's performance improved substantially, and

the managers of the company were making better decisions and driving value creation for the investor.

Figure 1–3 illustrates Acme's value creation relative to the S&P 400 before and after their adoption of value management as an operating mind-set within the company.

Acme Electronics manufactures electronic components and sells them to customers in a variety of industries. The company's manufacturing processes require a substantial investment in capital equipment, and product quality is an important consideration, as are production volume and manufacturing yield. The company is not a technology leader but does invest in R&D to stay current with its product line.

Acme has multiple divisions. One division is the Commodity Components Division (CCD). This division manufactures and sells products to telecommunications, computers, and networking companies. In 1992, the Commodity Components Division was earning a profit of $25 million per year on annual sales of $300 million. The division employs 2,000 people making 6,000 products.

Management was very concerned about the profitability level of the division and wanted to understand how they could improve CCD's performance. They previously tried reengineering, reduced the workforce with several rounds of layoffs, and reduced operating expenses. However, management perceived that the division was still lagging behind the competition in profitability. In short, CCD was underperforming relative to its industry, and its strategy focused on volume as a way to achieve cost advantages through scale.

In 1992, CCD became interested in managing for value. Much of the emphasis for this initiative came from the new general manager of the CCD division, who was under pressure from Acme's CEO to improve performance. The general manager wanted fast results and decided to begin by improving his management team's understanding of the

FIGURE 1-3

Relative Value of $100 Invested in Acme in December 1991: Acme vs. the S&P Industrials

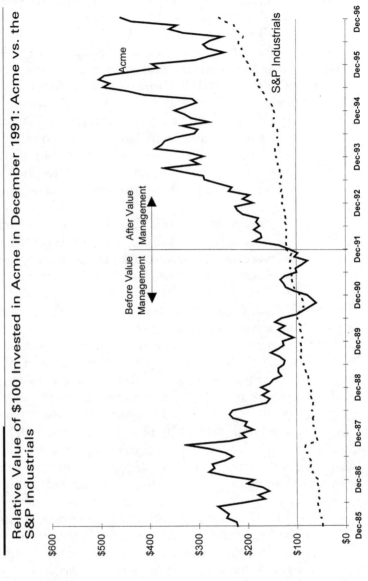

division's competitive position. He began by commissioning an analysis of the division's current competitive position to improve his understanding of CCD's competitive situation. A number of critical attributes for success in the market were identified. These attributes were the issues the customers felt were most important in making the decision to buy CCD's products. The study was not limited to existing CCD customers but also included past customers and customers of other suppliers to achieve a balanced understanding of CCD's strengths and weaknesses. One of the first objectives of the study was to determine what CCD's customers thought was important (as opposed to what CCD thought was important to the customers). Table 1–1 lists the attributes customers identified.

Having identified the key attributes of the customers' decision, the study went on to determine where CCD stood on each attribute relative to the two largest competitors. The results of the analysis showed that CCD had the lowest price but lagged behind in a number of other key attributes. Figure 1–4 shows CCD's competitive position relative to its two prime competitors for each of the key attributes.

From this data, it is apparent that CCD was competitively disadvantaged and overly reliant on price for competitive differentiation. These results were quite different

T A B L E   1–1

Key Performance Attributes

Low price
Support
Quality
Delivery
"Safe buy"
R&D

F I G U R E   1–4

Relative Capabilities of Acme vs. Competitors

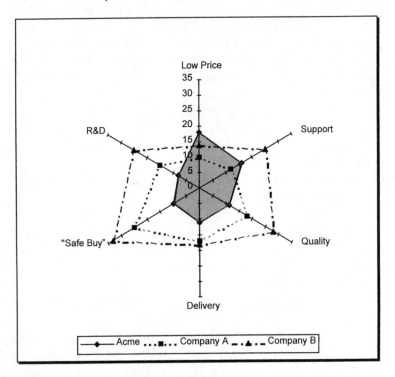

Note: The further out on each axis, the better -- the company with the greatest area enclosed by its "web of attributes" has the best competitive position.

from management's beliefs about CCD's position and demonstrated a much larger gap in competitive position than management realized.

In addition to the findings of the customer analysis, the study discovered that CCD had many more product lines than the competition. This was contributing to enormous inefficiencies, especially during periods of peak demand. During these periods, manufacturing time was split between the different product lines, resulting in substantial manufacturing set-up costs and inefficiencies that lead to higher overall costs of production. CCD also had to carry more inventory than competitors to fill customer orders across its broad product line.

Not only was CCD supporting more product lines than the competition, the revenue per product line was lagging behind the competition. In a capital-intensive business where the fixed costs must be amortized across the production runs, the low revenue per product line was generating a serious cost disadvantage. Table 1–2 summarizes CCD's status before the introduction of value management.

This situation needed to change if CCD was going to improve its competitive position and profitability. To better understand how to improve performance, CCD first identified the three major segments of their business: telecommu-

TABLE 1–2

Why did the Commodity Components Business Unit Introduce the Managing for Value Process (MVP)?

Competitive Issue	CCD's Position Before MVP
Financial performance (vs. competitors)	Underperformer
Primary focus	Volume
Source of increased profits	Across-the-board cost cutting
Business planning	Very limited/historical extrapolations
Competitor intelligence	Limited
Business objectives	Conflicting
Employees' perceived ability to influence results	Low
Management incentives	Subjective, not linked to strategy
Production capacity	Constrained
Product line profitability	Numerous cross-subsidies

nications, computers, and networking. CCD then analyzed their competitive position and the market economics of these customer segments. Based on their improved understanding of the business developed earlier in the customer and financial analysis, CCD was able to graphically depict their competitive position.

The analysis shown in Figure 1–5 identifies CCD's different customer segments and their relative positions in terms of the attractiveness of the customer market segments. Can CCD earn a profit? How well positioned is CCD relative to its competition in meeting the needs of the customers and earning a return on the investment it has in the business?

In CCD's case, the networking customer segment is very attractive, and CCD is benefiting from strong market economics. CCD is competitively advantaged because they entered this segment early and gained an early toehold with their technology. Over the years, they leveraged the technology into a large market share and found the market economics for this segment to be very appealing. CCD has the advantage of technology capabilities, economies of scale, and experience that their competitors do not. The result is an attractive business for CCD.

The story is similar in telecommunications. The market economics are attractive, and CCD was able to generate a strong position with their customers and maintain customer loyalty because of their low cost and highly responsive service. CCD also manufactured customized components for these customers on an as-needed basis. This led to CCD's advantage over competitors.

Unlike the case in the networking and telecommunications markets, however, CCD entered the computer market later than its competitors. The market economics in this segment are not attractive because there is little technological advantage for any of the competitors, and any cost advantages are generally passed on to the customer in the

FIGURE 1-5

Did CCD Focus on Volume Before Introducing the Managing for Value Process?

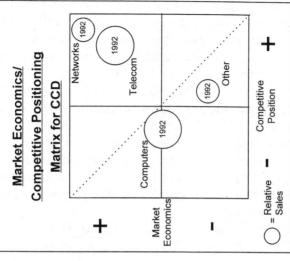

Market Economics/ Competitive Positioning Matrix for CCD

Networks (1992)

1992 — Telecom

Computers (1992)

(1992) Other

Market Economics

+ –

Competitive Position

+ –

◯ = Relative Sales

Market Economics/Competitive Positioning (ME/CP) framework was developed and popularized by Marakon Associates.

CCD's Focus on Volume

- Focus on sales volume growth dominated

- Discounting tactics contributed to industry price war, e.g.,
  - "Buy one, get one free"
  - Volume discounts
  - Discounting
  - Price concessions

- Major issue -- How to increase average prices?

15

form of lower prices. This makes it difficult to earn attractive returns in this business. CCD is competitively disadvantaged in this market segment because of their late entry and because, unlike their competitors, they are not as innovative; any returns the competitors earn as a function of new technology are difficult for CCD to match.

Although CCD prided itself on being a low-cost manufacturing operation, nothing could have been further from the truth. The cost of the typical product manufactured by CCD was 23 percent higher than that of the average competitor. This information was particularly disturbing to the CCD management team because it demonstrated that the strategy of low cost based on volume was not achieving the objective.

The problem was in the lack of focus and the number of product lines CCD was attempting to support and run through their manufacturing operation. This proliferation of products was the source of the cost disadvantage and the lackluster profitability of the division. In the name of customer service, CCD had allowed itself to proliferate product lines without sufficient thought to the associated costs. The costs in this case were insidious and came in the form of more manufacturing changes, shorter production runs, scheduling bottlenecks, and higher inventory levels. From a cost perspective, these costs led to CCD being less competitive than they originally thought.

VALUE MANAGEMENT AT CCD

CCD used value management to introduce the value mind-set into its decision making. Managing for value meant cutting back on the number of product lines to focus the energies of the division on only a few areas where they had competitive advantage that could be built upon or maintained. After discussing the problem and identifying the opportunity to create value, management agreed upon value creation as the goal. Management agreed that they would evaluate decisions by the amount of value each decision created. CCD also changed their strategic planning, budgeting/resource allocation, and incentive compensation so that these processes were both aligned with the goal of creating value and were consistent with one another.

Division managers in CCD believed the results from value management were worth the effort because their decision to manage for value paid off handsomely. For the next four years, CCD led the rest of the company in performance, and Acme created more value for investors than either its peers or the stock market as measured by the S&P 500. The results are shown in Figure 1–6.

CCD's performance improved a great deal, and Acme outperformed its peers. Yet, the changes that resulted from value management were more profound than a single period's financial results. Table 1–3 compares CCD along a number of attributes before and after value management took hold in the division.

Value management is an important management tool that can be used to create a mind-set for good decision making and improved performance. It creates the right balance between short- and long-term decisions and helps management balance the trade-offs between improved levels of profit and greater growth. The remaining chapters in this book will provide an in-depth discussion of value management. They will explain what value management is and what it is not. They will provide examples of companies that have managed for value as well as those that have failed to do so. In addition, the steps required for successful implementation of a value management program will be explained.

18

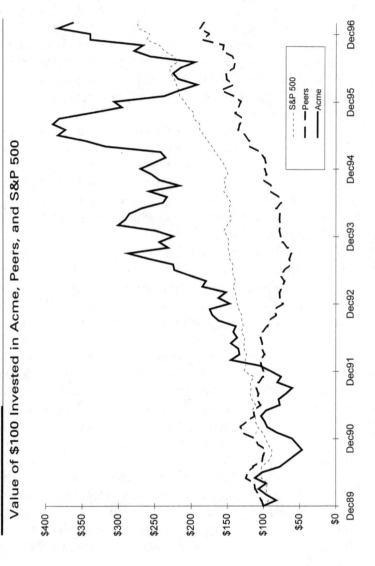

FIGURE 1-6

Value of $100 Invested in Acme, Peers, and S&P 500

T A B L E 1-3

What Are the Major Benefits of the Managing For Value Process to CCD?

	Before MVP	After MVP
(1) Financial performance (vs. competitors)	Underperformer	Outperform
(2) Primary focus	Volume	Focus on advantaged products
(3) Source of increased profits	Across-the-board cost cutting	Profitable
(4) Business planning	Historical extrapolations	Fact-based "bottom-up" plan & valuation of alternatives
(5) Competitor intelligence	Limited	Significant
(6) Business objectives	Conflicting	Aligned
(7) Employees perceived ability to influence results	Low	High
(8) Management incentives	Arbitrary, not linked to strategy	Linked to strategy
(9) Cross-product line profitability	Numerous cross-subsidies	Measurable profitability

CHAPTER 2

Value Creation

WHAT IS VALUE CREATION?

Value creation is the wealth created for a company's stockholders through price appreciation and dividends. We can calculate the value created by any public company for any time period in percentage terms, equity capitalization, indexed to dollars invested, or on a per-share basis. There are advantages and disadvantages to each approach, but the idea is the same: Measure the amount of value created for shareholders over a certain period of time. Figure 2–1 presents four methods applied to IBM for 1996. In each calculation, we start with the same basic facts:

Share price at beginning of the period	$91⅜
Dividends paid	$1.40
Share price at the end of the period	$151½

Even though it can be calculated in a variety of ways, value created is a straightforward idea. In cases where a stock price is readily available in the public market and dividend

22

F I G U R E 2–1

IBM Value Creation in 1996

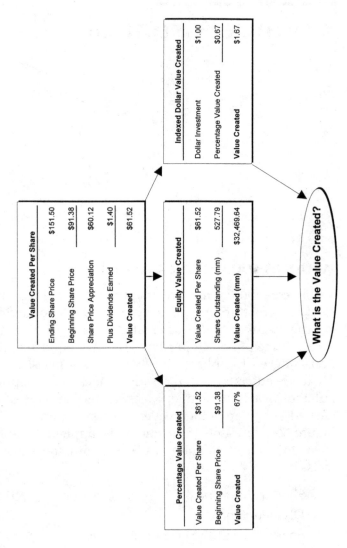

Value Created Per Share	
Ending Share Price	$151.50
Beginning Share Price	$91.38
Share Price Appreciation	$60.12
Plus Dividends Earned	$1.40
Value Created	$61.52

Percentage Value Created	
Value Created Per Share	$61.52
Beginning Share Price	$91.38
Value Created	67%

Equity Value Created	
Value Created Per Share	$61.52
Shares Outstanding (mm)	527.79
Value Created (mm)	$32,469.64

Indexed Dollar Value Created	
Dollar Investment	$1.00
Percentage Value Created	$0.67
Value Created	$1.67

What is the Value Created?

payments can be obtained, calculating value created is a trivial exercise. Changes in capital structure and share issuance introduce some complexity, but the information is usually easily available. The answer is less obvious when looking at value to be created in the future. Figure 2–2 illustrates the difference between historical value created and value to be created in the future.

Value in the future is not always easy to calculate because there are different perspectives on what value is or should be. To begin the discussion about value, we will initially limit ourselves to stock market value. Later, we will examine other types of value.

Value usually implies a mathematical calculation, which leads us to believe that value is objective. But is it? All value—past, present, and future—is actually subjective. We can look at the past values and agree on what they were because, for instance, we know IBM's stock price was quoted on December 31, 1996, as $151½ per share. This information is not in dispute, so the observation of the value of IBM on that date appears to be objective. But the value itself is subjective because the value of IBM shares on the last day of December in 1996 was nothing more than the value of the stock traded between the last two investors on that date. *Value* is therefore an imprecise term whose analysis is more art than science.

Stock market value is the net present value of the expected sequence of future cash flows the company will generate for the equity holders of the company. This expression of value can be represented by the following mathematical equation:

$$\text{Value} = \sum_{t=Today}^{\infty} PV \text{ Equity cash flow}_t, \text{ where}$$

$$PV \text{ Equity cash flow}_t = \frac{\text{Cash flow}_t}{(1 + r)^t}$$

using r as the discount rate.

FIGURE 2-2

IBM Stock Price—High, Low, and Close

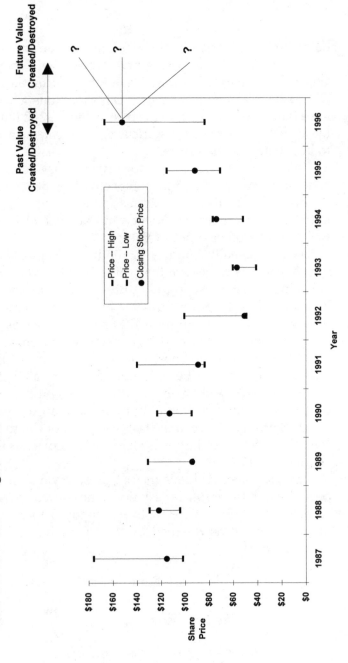

This equation states that the stock market places a value today on the present value of the stream of anticipated future cash flows available to equity holders. These cash flows include not only dividends but reinvestments of the future cash flows in the company. This definition is a simplification that depends on knowledge of future cash flows. The question is, "What are the future cash flows?" There is no one right answer because we do not know in advance what the future cash flows will be. This leads to multiple interpretations of future cash flows and the values they imply.

Value has a variety of meanings, and people can have very different views of what the value of a company is at any given point in time. They may disagree on today's value or on the future value. This dynamic of different views of value plays itself out every day in the securities markets where buyers and sellers declare their beliefs about companies' values through the actions they take to buy or sell the stock. They buy when they believe value is greater than the value represented by the price in the market, and they sell when they believe the value is less than the value represented in the market. Market price is a value that all owners of stock feel is not too high and that all potential owners feel is not too low.

VALUE IS SUBJECTIVE

The expression of past value appears objective. However, present value or future value have much greater room for disagreement because the value judgment becomes nonobservable and subjective. Figure 2–3 illustrates the different views of value.

Value is in the eyes of the beholder, which is why there can be a variety of opinions about value, and each of them can be correct. A variety of factors contribute to these perspectives, including an individual's:

- Quality of information.
- Perception of control.
- Time horizon.
- Uncertainty.
- Tolerance for risk.

These factors create the individual's perspective on the value of a particular company at a given time. Because perceptions are dynamic and change over time, an individual's view of value today may be different from his or her view of value tomorrow.

FIGURE 2-3

Different Views of Value

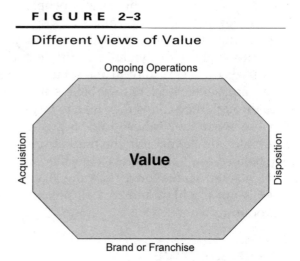

Ongoing Operations

Acquisition

Value

Disposition

Brand or Franchise

INFORMATION

Information is the most powerful single factor in determining value and the greatest explanation for different values. Information about the past is objective, but information about the future is subjective. Further, different people have different information.

One way of demonstrating the power of information

as a determinant of value is to examine the trading range of IBM in 1996. During the year, the stock traded as low as $83 per share and as high as $166 per share. If we multiply IBM's share price at its 1996 low and its high times the average shares outstanding (531 million), we get a range of total value for IBM's equity of $44.1 billion to $87.6 billion.[1] Was the value of the company that different between January and December?

The difference in the values at those two dates is the difference in what investors were willing to pay for IBM based on their perceptions of value at those two times. The information about IBM and its business prospects changed during the year because IBM was emerging from a turn-around in their business, and investors were adjusting their beliefs about IBM's value upward as the turnaround became more and more complete and the information about IBM's positive results were more generally available.

Information is not always uniformly available. One investor may have information that another does not have concerning the company's likely future sales. Another investor may have access to analyst reports on the industry. Management of the company is likely to have different information than outside investors have. Some of the differences in value are the results of these different amounts of information. For example, management may know more about a company's prospects than the typical investor and might therefore attach a higher value than the typical investor.

PERCEPTION OF CONTROL

The second greatest determinant of value is the investor's perception of control. If you take two individuals and offer them the same opportunity to make money in an uncertain environment but give one the perception that she can control or influence the outcome, the individual to whom you gave the perception of control will almost always pay more for the opportunity than the individual who believes the outcome is uncertain and that he has no control.

Insiders usually believe they have more control over the future events in a company and of the outcome that company will generate, rather than outsiders. As a result, insiders are likely to pay more for the company than individuals without any perceived control over the company's future.

TIME HORIZON

Different time horizons also influence value. If your time horizon is the next fiscal quarter, your perception of value will be very different than someone with a 10-year time horizon. One of the interesting questions inquires into the appropriate time horizon on which to focus the company's managers. Today, many management teams are very heavily focused on short-term results and focus on a time horizon of a single quarter. Is this what investors want? Some investors must, or management would not respond to short-term pressure.

Management can easily fall into the trap of focusing only on the current quarter in the mistaken belief that investors only care about this quarter's financial results. The corporate world is full of short-term thinking, thinking that is costing companies enormous opportunities because short-term current quarter thinking discourages growth investments and handicaps the company competitively.

UNCERTAINTY

How certain is the value? What does the value depend on? If the value today is the expectation of future financial results, how sure are we about those expected results? The greater the uncertainty about future results, the greater the variance in the potential value. Uncertainty works both ways, acting either to reduce or increase value. In most cases, reduction is more likely (with the prominent exception of values in high technology where uncertainty actually becomes a positive), and so the greater the uncertainty about future results, the lower the value is likely to be. Uncertainty is a subjective judgment about those future results. No one knows what the future results will be; if they did, there would be no uncertainty. Without the certainty of future results, investors are likely to discount the future results by some factor in setting their expectations for the value of the company. The greater the uncertainty about the future results, the greater the discount investors will place on the future results.

TOLERANCE FOR RISK

Two investors can have the same information, perception of control, and uncertainty about future prospects yet still place different values on the company because they themselves have different tolerances for risk. Those investors who are more tolerant of risk, who have a high tolerance for uncertainty, will pay a higher value for a company with uncertain prospects than will an investor who is less tolerant of risk.

TYPES OF VALUES

Value in the present and future is subjective, but that does not mean it cannot be quantified. The value, when quantified, is based on our beliefs about a number of factors. The value we are willing to pay reflects our beliefs about each of these factors at a given time. The beliefs may change; if they do, so will the value. Let's expand the discussion beyond market value and look at other types of value:

- Ongoing operating value
- Discounted cash flow (DCF)
- Net present value (NPV)
- Plan value
- Disposal value
- Fire-sale value
- Book value
- Market value added
- Brand value

- Franchise value
- Intellectual capital value
- Acquisition value
- Fair market value
- Going concern value
- Forced-sale value
- Goodwill value
- Enterprise value
- Liquidation value

Many types of value represent investors' views of value under different circumstances and assumptions. The types of value can be grouped by the uncertainties and assumptions that drive the definitions of value. The stock market incorporates these different views of value into the market price through individuals' actions to buy or sell based on their beliefs about future cash flows. The following discussion will highlight key definitions of value, outlining their varied uses and interpretations.

Ongoing operating value and plan value are based on the future cash flows of the business. Ongoing operating value is, as the name implies, the value of the business, assuming it will continue to operate. This is similar to market value in most respects and involves judgments about the value of the cash flows going forward in time and the need to replace the existing assets with other productive assets at some future date(s). There may be different expectations about the cash flows in the operations going forward in time, but the ongoing operating value assumes the existing assets will be used to generate future cash flows and will not be sold. Investors consider the value of ongoing operations and compare it to the value of the assets if production is terminated. Operating the business makes sense if the operating value exceeds the terminating value. Plan value is also an expression of ongoing value. It is the value of management's plan and is based on the future cash flows and investments specified in the plan, combined with an ongoing operating value at the end of the plan's time horizon.

Disposal and fire-sale or liquidation values are asset-driven values and depend on how much someone is willing to pay for the assets. Disposal value looks at the company from the perspective that the assets will be sold and usually imposes a discount on the cash flows the business is able to generate. The fire-sale value is similar to the disposal value, but in addition to assuming the assets are to be sold, it assumes the assets must be sold quickly to raise cash.

Book value represents the investors' equity contributions to the business as captured by the accounting books. This perspective on value is limited by what has happened in the past. It is the reflection of all past investments, financing, and operating decisions and provides a view of value as the cumulative effect of prior events while remaining mute on future prospects.

Market value added is a term in use today that is often misunderstood. Market value added is the measurement of the company's market value in excess of the company's book value. This measure of value tells us how much more than accounting value investors are willing to pay for the company. Theoretically, it is also the sum of all future streams of economic value added. But it is usually quoted as market value less book value and can be highly misleading when used for comparison purposes. Since it relies on accounting value, it represents the difference between market value and book value. If book value is distorted, market value added will be as well.

Companies that rely heavily on their brand names to produce cash flow often talk about value in terms of brand or franchise values. These values are confusing because they can mean one of two things. First, the brand value is the ability of the company's brands to earn above cost-of-capital returns on the investments in those brands. Second, brand value can also mean the value of the brand to a potential acquirer of the brand. Brand value is a mix of these two perspectives, one operating related and the other acquisition or divestiture related.

Intellectual capital value represents the company's future cash flows that will be derived from the investments the company has made in knowledge capabilities and people. This intellectual capital may show up for customers in future products or services offered. Often, research and development expenditures are discussed in terms of intellectual capital. Intellectual capital is the most intangible and most difficult of the value terms to quantify and therefore is typically subject to a great deal of debate. Some proponents of intellectual capital suggest capturing its value in accounting statements. This suggestion is interesting, but measuring the value of intellectual capital with precision is highly problematic because of the uncertainty surrounding the precise definition of intellectual capital and the various methods of calculating it.

Acquisition values are the value of the business to someone else. Sometimes the value of a business can be greater to an outside group of investors or another company because of the decisions they could make if they owned the business to create value or as a function of the investor's ability to generate more cash flow from economies of scale or of scope. Leveraged buyouts are examples of cases where investor groups believe they can create more value than the current owners.

Take Wells Fargo's acquisitions, for example. The banks that Wells Fargo acquired were more valuable to Wells Fargo than to the selling shareholders. The increase in value resulted from Wells Fargo's use of its systems to reduce costs and earn greater returns from the acquired bank's assets than the acquired bank was earning on its own.

The ability to effect change is another value that may not involve an acquisition. Louis Gerstner, when he took over as CEO of IBM, placed a higher value on the company than the stock market did because he believed he would be able to change the fortunes of the company. His belief in his ability to change the company led him to value the company more highly than other shareholders did. Consequently, in addition to his salary he asked for, and received, a large grant of stock options in the company, options that would only be valuable to him if he was indeed able to change the company.

INFORMATION CONTROLS VALUE

What an investor expects to happen to the company's cash flows is the largest determinant of value, and as we have discussed, a variety of factors contribute to that perception. Value is always based on expectations of the future and is difficult to quantify even for public companies. For private companies where the information is not as readily available, the task is even more difficult.

On any given day, we can discover part of what people believe about future prospects by looking at the market price of a company's shares. Market price is an indicator of what people's beliefs are because at any given time the value as quoted by the offered price of shares represents the lowest marginal value a holder is willing to accept in return for a share of the company's stock. This tells us that the value placed on the shares by all other holders of the company's stock is greater than the offered price. The bid price represents the converse, the highest marginal value an investor is willing to pay for shares in the company stock. All other buyers are willing to pay that price or less for the company's shares. Investors are indicating their beliefs in their decisions to buy or sell because these decisions represent their beliefs about the company's prospects.

Value, then, is a subjective statement of beliefs about the future and represents a perception (one of many possible perceptions) about the company's prospects. Market price is the value at which all holders and nonholders are satisfied.

MARKET EFFICIENCY AND THE TYRANNY OF INVESTORS

Markets are efficient, or so most economists would have us believe. Efficient market theory tells us that the market has available information, and investors make rational judgments based on that information to set the market prices for stocks. At any given time, the market represents the informed judgment of all investors, and it is therefore impossible to "beat-the-market" and deliver excess returns to investors using available information.

If the theory of market efficiency is true, this is good news for managers. If the market is efficient, the company's shares are priced fairly at any given time, and managers who make good decisions that improve cash flow and prospects or that reduce risk and discount rates will exceed market expectations for returns to shareholders. The good news for managers who are working to add value is that the market will reflect what they do.

Consider the following story. Allegedly, one day Warren Buffett and Milton Friedman were walking down the street in Chicago. Buffett spotted a $10 bill lying in the gutter and stooped to pick it up. Friedman grabbed him by the arm to stop him and said, "If the $10 bill were real, someone would already have picked it up." This story provides a quick illustration of market efficiency and why market efficiency is anathema to most managers. Managers want to believe that opportunities exist to create value and that they can create value for their shareholders. Gerstner certainly held this belief when he went to IBM.

Empirical evidence suggests that the information available to individual companies is usually imperfect. Imperfect information may take the form of changing customer habits that will lead a company to competitive advantages or disadvantages, or a company may be able to improve its manufacturing efficiencies faster than other companies realize.

There are an infinite number of ways the information about a company may not be perfect; each of these is an opportunity that leaves plenty of room for managers to create value through the decisions they make and the way they deploy the company's resources. The market may be more efficient in pricing larger companies, with legions of stock analysts following their every move for a hint of their corporate fortunes. In total, the market is surprisingly efficient because the errors of over- and undervaluation in individual stocks balance out. Individual stocks may not be as efficiently priced due to imperfect or unavailable information. With this said, it is true that investors will price a stock to reflect their expectations for the future and in so far as their expectations exceed the current financial results, the challenge for management may be formidable.

THE ROLE OF MANAGEMENT

Value is stated in the present but is always based on future expectations and represents the subjective view of investors about the company's prospects. Determining the value of a company is an important activity, as is determining the value of the company's plan. For management, however, value is not an exercise in measurement but in decisions. The role of management is to create value for the shareholders.

Creating value for the shareholders means creating value that meets or exceeds their expectations for value creation. As we have seen, investors have expectations concerning value, which are evidenced in the way they value the company's stock. If investors expect the future cash flows of a company to be $50 million, management's job is to maximize value. If management can beat the investors expectations, so much the better. But suppose the best management can do is deliver cash flows of $40 million. In this case, management's job is still to maximize value. This means a reduced market price when investors discover that their expectations exceeded management's ability to deliver.

Management may find itself in a position where the probability of beating the investors' expectations is low. This is a problem. The point can be illustrated by an actual company whose investors' expectations exceeded the company's ability to deliver. For the previous five years, this company earned returns below its cost of capital. The stock is now trading at a value of $31 per share with 150 million shares outstanding, representing a market value of $4.6 billion. The company is generating a cash flow of $350 million per year. Investors must be expecting improved returns to justify the market value of $4.6 billion. If you assume the current cash flow went on as a steady stream with a 12 percent cost of capital discount rate, it only justifies a market value of $3 billion, or $19.50 per share, while the stock is trading at $31. Therefore, to explain a stock price of $31 per share, investors must be expecting returns to improve. The difference between $31 per share and $19.50 represents the improvement investors are expecting in the returns of the business.

From a quick analysis, it looks as though investors are expecting cash flow to increase from $350 million today to $760 million within five years to explain the valuation on the stock. When you compare and contrast the company's long-range plan with these expectations, you find a large disconnection between what investors are expecting and the returns management is planning to generate. This disconnection leads to a potential problem for the management team because even if they perfectly execute their long-range plan, they are going to disappoint investors who are expecting higher returns. The gap is shown graphically in Figure 2–4.

Management's role is to maximize true value or what the market would find to be true value if it had access to all information about the company's operations. In addition, management needs to manage the expectations of investors so they don't get ahead of the company's ability to deliver results. These issues are two sides of the same coin. Management that correctly sets investor expectations is more likely to meet or exceed those expectations than management that allows investors' expectations to get out of balance with the company's ability to deliver.

But meeting or beating investors' expectations begs the question of over what time frame investors are expecting returns. All too often management focuses on the short-term results at the expense of future opportunities. This is done under the guise of meeting quarterly earnings expectations. But management should ask itself a simple question: "What is my investors' average time horizon?" Not all investors in companies are quarterly momentum stock players. The vast majority of stock is held in long-term hands, yet management feels pressured to deliver for the investors who have the shortest time horizon. Does this make sense? Do a thorough analysis of the holders of your company's stock to determine if your investors really want you to maximize quarterly earnings. The likely answer, based on the studies we've done, is that they want you to manage the quarterly earnings for consistency, but they have invested in the company and the management team to bring them returns over the long term. Check it out; you might be surprised by the results.

Recently, a Fortune 100 CEO asked us to explain why he was receiving so much pressure from investors for quarterly returns and to explore whether or not he had enough flexibility with investors to deliver slightly lower earnings

FIGURE 2-4

Planned Cash Flow vs. Expectations

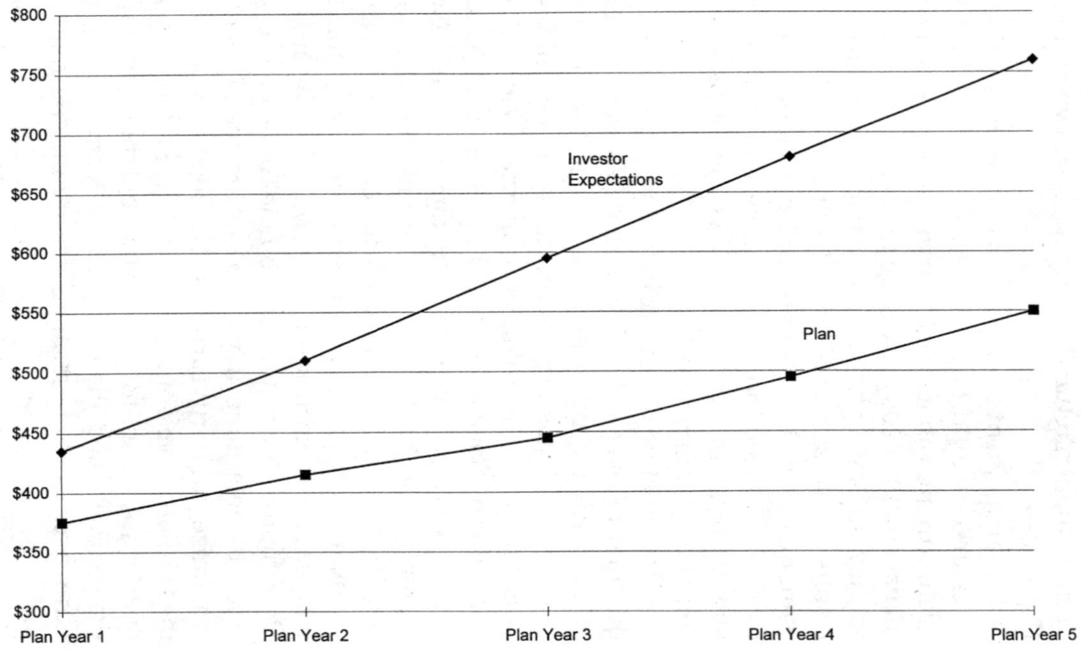

for a year in return for an important capital commitment he wanted to make. The results of the analysis were surprising. We discovered that over 85 percent of the stock in his company was in long-term hands (defined as three or more years). The remaining 15 percent of the stock was held by a group of "fast money" mutual funds that were calling him weekly to apply not-so-subtle pressure to maximize quarterly earnings in the near term to try and drive the stock price up. Figure 2–5 shows the results of the analysis. With a higher comfort level, knowing that most of his investors were interested in more than just quarterly returns, the CEO went ahead and made the investment that he thought was in the best interest of the company. The stock price soared the following year as the results of the successful new capital investment were disseminated to investors.

THE SLIPPERY SLOPE OF VALUE CREATION

Just because a company is highly profitable does not guarantee value creation for investors in the company. Creating value for shareholders operates under three rules:

1. Level of profitability has nothing to do with value creation. When it comes to creating value for shareholders, companies that are very profitable have no advantage over companies that are less profitable.

2. All management teams start on a level playing field for creating value.

3. Different companies face different challenges in creating value. Companies are handicapped (like in golf) based on results to date.

These three rules are the slippery slope of value creation. No matter how good you get at creating value, investors will realize it and price your stock accordingly, which will make it correspondingly more difficult for you to create

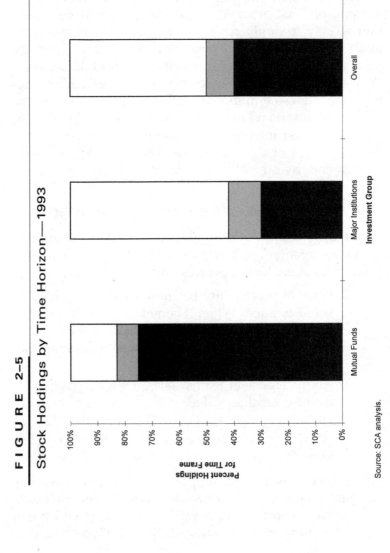

F I G U R E   2-5

Stock Holdings by Time Horizon—1993

Source: SCA analysis.

value in the future. This reassessment of the degree of difficulty in creating incremental value is what levels the playing field between companies. By increasing the stock price, investors are giving management credit for performance to date, but they are also increasing the degree of difficulty in creating future value.

Figure 2–6 separates companies in the S&P 500 into quartiles by their level of profitability. There is no relationship between the level of profitability and the returns those companies earned for their investors in subsequent periods. This is good news for management because the starting point in profitability does not matter; it's what you do to improve the results that matters.

For example, Figure 2–7 shows Intel creating value for investors from 1989 to 1993 by increasing its operating returns from 9 to 24 percent. Investors repriced the stock accordingly. To continue generating returns in excess of the investors' expectations, management needs to improve returns from 24 percent to a higher plateau and/or grow the business. This is likely to be more difficult. The task of consistently creating value becomes more and more difficult the better you get. Consequently, the playing field may not be level in the sense of degree of difficulty required to achieve improved results. However, there are companies that have created value year after year. The largest example over the last 10 years is Coca-Cola. Many lesser-known companies have also consistently created value for their investors. We'll take a look at some examples in later chapters.

Remember, the question investors are asking is "What have you done for me lately?" You may have improved operating returns, but investors gave you credit for that by increasing the value of the company. Now they want to know what you're going to do to create more value.

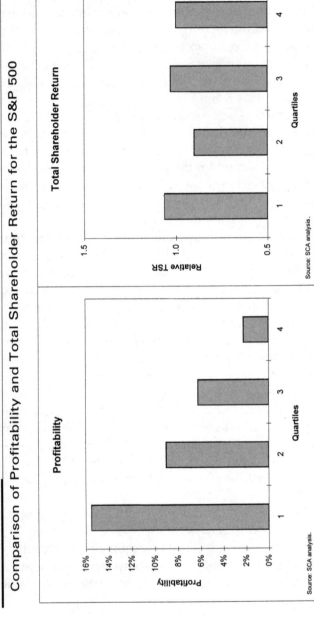

FIGURE 2-6

Comparison of Profitability and Total Shareholder Return for the S&P 500

Value of $100 Invested in Intel Corporation

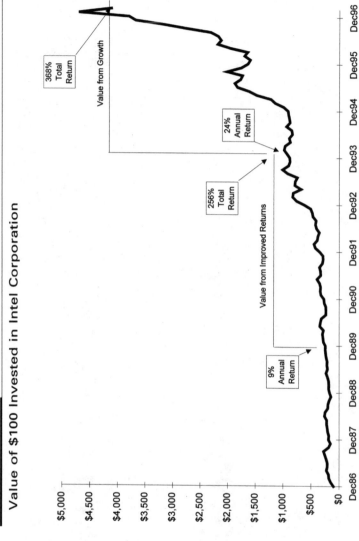

CHAPTER 3

Why Manage
for Value?

Security analysts, boards of directors, and shareholders are putting a great deal of pressure on management to increase shareholder value. In addition to this pressure from investors and their agents, there are numerous good reasons to manage for value, including the following:

- To prevent undervaluation of the stock.
- To facilitate communication with investors and analysts.
- To encourage value-creating investments.
- To improve resource allocation.
- To streamline planning and budgeting.
- To set more effective targets for planning and compensation.
- To balance short- and long-term trade-offs.
- To set management priorities.
- To improve decision making.
- To improve internal strategy communication.
- To serve as a catalyst for change.

- To facilitate the use of stock for mergers and acquisitions.
- To prevent takeovers.
- To increase the value of stock options and incentives.

CREATING VALUE CONSISTENTLY

Some companies create much more value for their share-holders than others, and the pressure is on other companies to do the same. Most published studies on value creation focus on how companies compare to one another by creating value for their investors relative to a broad market index such as the Standard and Poor's 500 (S&P 500) in the United States or the Financial Times 100 (FTSE 100) in the United Kingdom. These comparisons are meaningful, but they obscure the important question of how well the company is doing for its shareholders relative to other companies in the same industry. Industry comparison is meaningful because cyclical or regulated companies can't be looked at for value creation in the same way as, for example, consumer products companies.

Figure 3–1 illustrates that very few companies outperform their industry averages over time. The vertical axis is the percentage of companies. The horizontal axis is the number of years in the last 10 that companies have outperformed their industry in creating value for their shareholders. The columns plotted are the number of companies that have outperformed their industry medians based on a sample of 750 Value Line companies. For example, from 1986 to 1995, only 13 percent of the companies outperformed their industry for at least 7 of the 10 years, while 100 percent outperformed their industry median in at least 1 year.

Outperforming your industry median in any given year is easy, but doing it consistently year after year is

FIGURE 3-1

Percentage of Companies Outperforming their Industry Median

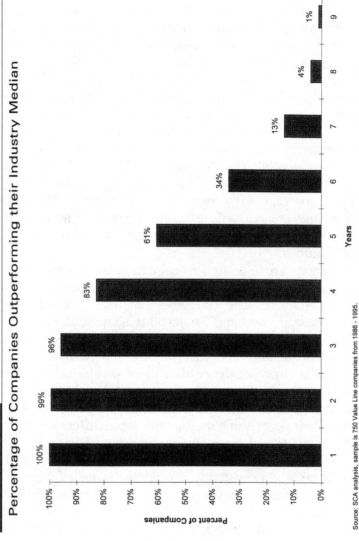

Source: SCA analysis, sample is 750 Value Line companies from 1986 - 1995.

difficult. Figure 3–1 shows just how difficult it is to consistently outperform the industry.

Although the number of companies consistently outperforming their industry average is small, the few companies that do consistently outperform their industries create a great deal of value. Figure 3–2 shows how much value was created by these consistent performers as measured by the value of $100 invested. What is the difference between these consistent performers and run-of-the-mill companies? How great a difference is there between companies that consistently create value and those that create value but not as consistently? The difference, as seen in Figure 3–2, is striking. The consistent value-creating company created $1600 for each $100 investment. In contrast, the median company created only $400 for each $100 invested. The value of consistently outperforming the industry is significant indeed.

In Figure 3–2, the vertical axis is the amount of value created relative to the industry median. The message here is important because it suggests that, over time, consistency is more important and beneficial to shareholders than one-time, value-creating events such as restructuring, financial engineering, and reengineering.

It is no coincidence that these companies do better. What separates these companies from the pack is that they are managed for value. One reason they consistently outperform their peers is that they are managed differently because they focus on creating value for investors. They achieve this focus by aligning their management teams to understand, focus on, and execute their business strategies. Figure 3–3 compares these companies to the broader S&P 500 market index.

In the next chapter, we'll take a look at what it means to be managed for value, but for now let's look at the same value-creation data another way and compare the one-time value creators with the consistent value creators. The one-

Value of $100 Invested Created by Consistent Value Creators

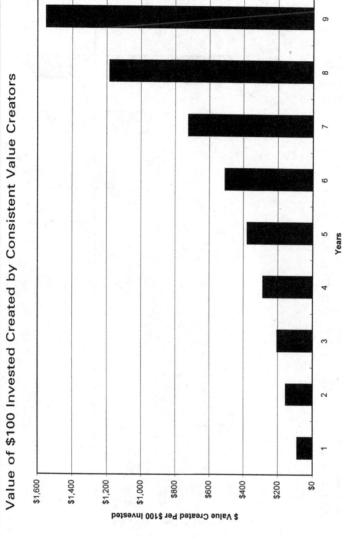

Source: SCA analysis, sample is 750 Value Line companies from 1986 - 1995.

49

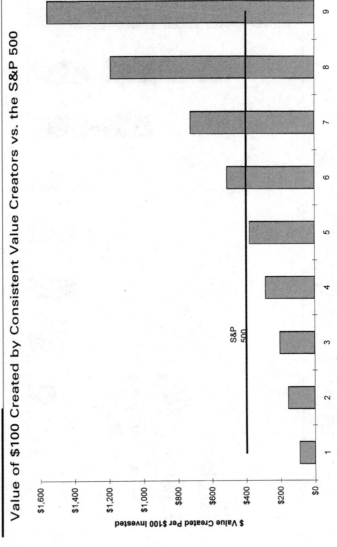

FIGURE 3-3

Value of $100 Created by Consistent Value Creators vs. the S&P 500

$ Value Created Per $100 Invested

$1,600
$1,400
$1,200
$1,000
$800
$600
$400
$200
$0

S&P 500

1 2 3 4 5 6 7 8 9

Years Outperforming Industry

Source: SCA analysis, sample is 750 Value Line companies from 1986 - 1995.

time value creators created value through financial reengineering, restructuring, and similar actions. The consistent performers created value by improving the operations of their business, becoming more competitive, and growing.

Michael Hammer's recent book on restructuring suggests creating an organization in the future that is more complicated than it is manageable and that the restructuring required to create these complex organizations will create value.[1] Why increase complexity for the sake of reengineering when the fundamental issue of creating value surrounds the choice and execution of competitive strategy? Often, the result of reengineering is to improve returns, and improving returns is a value-creating activity. However, a focus solely on improving returns risks ignoring value-creating growth opportunities. Reengineering done to improve profits by cutting costs will, if successful, create value on a one-time basis. The real challenge is to create value consistently.

For the purpose of comparing one-time value creators with consistent value creators, let's choose some companies at random and look at which ones created value through one-time events and which ones did it through consistent operating performance. Some of the one-time value creators created value through changes in financial structure, such as leverage, asset sales, and so on. Others accomplished their one-time gains through reengineering the company. It is interesting to look at the long-term results for the shareholders. In this group of companies, one-time value creators created, on average, 62 percent of value relative to their peers. The consistent value creators, on the other hand, created 400 percent of the value of their peers.

Think of the differences between the one-time value creators and the ongoing value creators as the difference between managing the financing or rationalizing the investment in the business and managing the assets. It is easy to see that some companies have been very successful in creating value through financing changes, restructuring, and other one-time events. Let's leave the description of how to accomplish these feats to the investment bankers and reengineering consultants. Our focus is on describing how to improve management of the assets. One reason companies outperform consistently is that they are focused on helping their operating managers and corporate management improve the existing operations and make new investments that add value.

CHALLENGES IN VALUE CREATION

Today's companies confront four daunting challenges as they attempt to consistently create value:

1. Increased complexity.
2. Greater uncertainty and risk.
3. Time compression.
4. Conflicting priorities.

Managers are being asked to make the complex simple, reduce uncertainty and risk, speed decision making, and balance conflicting priorities. The challenges are daunting indeed. How can a manager balance the company's desire for growth expressed in the strategic plan with the CEO's pressure for quarterly results when any growth initiative will come at the expense of quarterly results? For example, if you build an additional facility, the depreciation charge will hit the quarterly results before the benefits do. If you expand your sales force to get closer to your customer, the expenses will hit the quarterly results before the sales force is fully functioning and productive. An acquisition will mean a hit to quarterly results for the cost of the acquisition and may even dilute earnings. Managers can easily be misled into believing that investments will destroy value and that growth is bad. In reality, there is good growth and bad growth. Good growth adds value, while bad growth destroys value. The trick is to identify good growth opportunities.

INCREASED COMPLEXITY

Managers are caught in a catch-22 where they have no reasonable way to make the trade-offs they are being asked to make. There is no way to satisfy all the conflicting goals. Against this backdrop of increased complexity is intensified competition. World markets are opening and trade is increasing, and maintaining a competitive position is becoming more and more difficult. Intensified competition demands quick decisions, yet managers are paralyzed by these trade-offs.

The challenge of sustaining value may be easier for companies in single product lines than for companies in multiple product lines because there is less complexity. Consider the example of Wm. Wrigley Jr. Company (the chewing gum company). Wrigley is essentially a single-product company with variations in the product line. Over the years, the company has added different flavors, introduced sugar-free gum, and developed other product innovations, extending the product line to keep pace with consumer demand and tastes. During this period, Wrigley created more value for the shareholders than most other companies. Figure 3–4 illustrates Wrigley's value creation for shareholders compared with the S&P 500 over the last 10 years.

The magic of Wrigley's success rests with two factors. The first is the family ownership of the business and William Wrigley's intense focus on the business. William Wrigley owns over 50 percent of the stock and takes a very value-oriented approach to management. His ownership allows the company to easily take a longer-term perspective. The second factor is the company's commitment to a single strategy that management understands.

Like Wrigley, Warren Buffett, CEO of Berkshire Hatha-

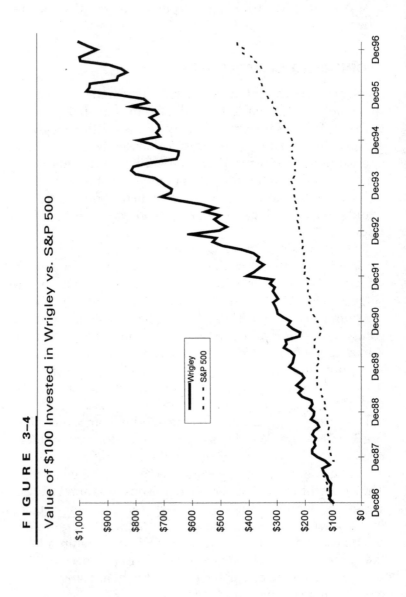

FIGURE 3-4

Value of $100 Invested in Wrigley vs. S&P 500

way, has also created enormous amounts of value for his shareholders. The results generated by Buffett are legendary in their proportions. Since 1987, he has generated a return in excess of 26 percent per year for shareholders (of which he is the largest). Buffett talks about understanding the businesses that he has invested in and reiterates his views in Berkshire Hathaway's annual report. His investments include Sees Candies, GEICO, Coca-Cola, and the *Washington Post*. These businesses share some of the same simplicity as the chewing gum business at Wrigley. If you want to know how Buffett creates value, you can pick up copies of the Berkshire Hathaway annual report and read the strategy he explains to his shareholders:[2]

1. Simple business (if there's lots of technology, we won't understand it).
2. Management in place (we can't supply it).
3. Businesses earning good returns on equity while employing little or no debt.
4. Demonstrated consistent earning power (future projections are of no interest to us, nor are "turnaround" situations).

GREATER UNCERTAINTY AND RISK

By contrast, Microsoft is in a more uncertain business where complexity abounds; creating value in the face of this complexity may be more complex. Yet Bill Gates has also delivered significant value to shareholders, as illustrated in Figure 3–5.

Microsoft's business complexity comes from multiple products, technical complexity, and a very uncertain product-development cycle. The rate of change in technology is faster than in almost any other industry, and Microsoft is faced with making decisions in this highly uncertain environment. Along with uncertainty comes risk, as Microsoft

56

FIGURE 3-5

Value of $100 Invested in Microsoft

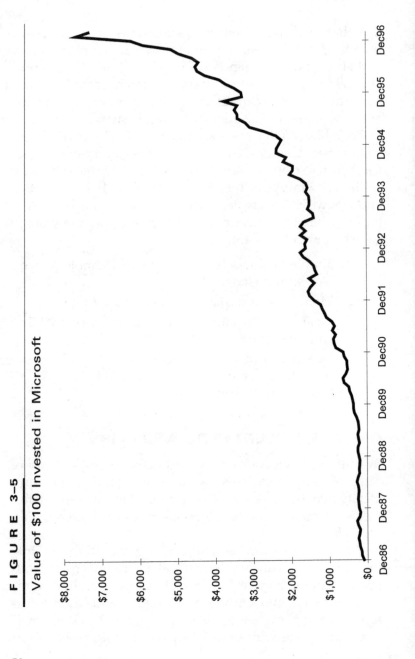

discovered when Netscape emerged with the Internet Navigator as an alternative to the virtual lock Microsoft held on the desktop operating system market.

TIME COMPRESSION

In addition to complexity and uncertainty, Microsoft and its peers also face the challenge of time compression. Time compression is the result of shortening technology life cycles, the need to bring new products to market faster, and customer-support demands that require 24-hour availability and quick response time. Time compression introduces another dimension of competition. The combination of these factors is depicted in Figure 3–6.

CONFLICTING PRIORITIES

Bill Gates is not alone. Together, these factors of complexity, uncertainty, and time compression provide the landscape against which many managers are being asked to make operating and investment decisions. This business landscape increases the chances that managers will need to balance and the conflicting priorities they will need to trade off as they consider alternatives. All companies are faced with conflicting priorities in the investment and operating decisions they make, but the more complex or uncertain the business, the greater the conflicts. A company such as Microsoft, which confronts an uncertain, complex environment where time compression is a driving factor, will face more conflicts than most.

These CEOs at Wrigley, Berkshire Hathaway, and Microsoft have one thing in common: They have defined what it takes to create value in their businesses, and they relentlessly execute against that strategy.

58

Complexity, Uncertainty, and Time Compression Lead to
Conflicting Priorities

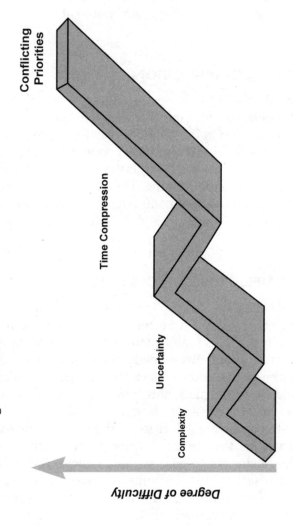

LESSONS FROM THE CONSISTENT PERFORMERS

If we look at the consistent value creators for clues about what they do differently to counter these formidable challenges, we find that these companies do three important things:

1. Capture the business strategy in the performance measures.
2. Pay management for value-creating performance.
3. Focus managers on the business strategy.

These are identifiable and transferable skills you can emulate and are applicable across industries, from retail to banking to airlines.

Capture the Business Strategy in the Performance Measures

This sounds straightforward and simple. Of course, you want to capture the business strategy in the performance measures, yet very few companies accomplish this goal. Most performance measures are financially oriented and focused on earnings per share and other, similar single-period financial performance measures.

Using performance measures to capture the business strategy, paying management for value-creating performance, and focusing managers on the business strategy is what separates excellent companies from typical companies. Excellent companies don't just measure results, they look beyond the results to the key drivers of their strategy and then include these drivers in the performance measures they use to measure how well they are doing against their strategic objectives. You remember the old axiom "What gets measured gets done." Well, if a company is measuring the increase in earnings per share, not the success of the business strategy, the results the company gets are likely to focus on earnings per share, not on the business strategy. Managers are likely to pay lip service to the business strategy while focusing on the performance measures, especially when the performance measures are tied to incentive compensation. Let's look at an example of a company that uses performance measures to support business strategy.

Dollar General is a $1.5 billion dollar retailer. The company has created value well above its peers, as Figure 3–7 illustrates. Dollar General is a good example of a company that captures their business strategy in the performance measures they use to capture their results. An excerpt from the 1995 annual report states,

> Dollar General continues to be successful because we keep things simple. The mission of Dollar General is serving others . . . serving customers, shareholders, and employees.

In retailing, the margins are razor thin because the average retailer earns 1.5 percent pretax on a dollar of sales. These razor-thin margins make cost control and cost advantage a major focus in the retail industry, and Dollar General has identified cost control as a key element of their business strategy. Management is determined to maintain a competitive cost position and build market share by passing on a portion of the cost savings to the consumer. Dollar General believes that by doing so they are creating a better value proposition for their customers and that this improved value proposition leads to more sales and higher profits. At the core of their lower cost strategy is a focus on holding down costs on repetitive tasks. The strategy contains the obvious cost elements of lower rental rates for their stores and managing employee costs. However, Dollar General goes further by identifying substantial hidden costs in the retail business.

These hidden costs are the result of business complexity. Complexity leads to higher costs through lower worker productivity and higher wage expenses. An example of a hidden cost is the productivity of labor. Higher employee

Value of $100 Invested in Dollar General vs. Peers (December 1986–December 1996)

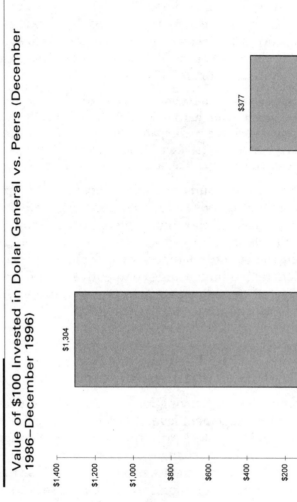

productivity translates into lower sales costs and lower wages as a percentage of sales. Dollar General says they are going to control the hidden costs of complexity and use this as a way to build competitive advantage into their business strategy, which is constructed by making each business process, from stocking the inventory to cash register sales, as simple as possible. Below, is a section of Dollar General's annual report for 1995:

> To remain true to the two-word mission of serving others, we've had to work hard to keep things simple. We look at ourselves as a family company where each member of the family—customers, shareholders, employees—shares in the success. To continue that success, we continue to simplify.

Let's examine the results of Dollar General's attempts to control both the obvious and hidden costs. Figure 3–8 illustrates Dollar General's position relative to their competitors in discount retail.

Using this subtle but important understanding of costs, Dollar General has built a large competitive cost advantage and translated the advantage into higher returns for the shareholders.

Pay Managers for Value-Creating Performance

Many companies are "paying for performance," especially at the senior management level. But the performance typically being paid for is stock price appreciation. Price appreciation, which includes changes in performance, discount rates, and expectations, creates problems when used as an incentive. The most common form of long-term incentive compensation today in public companies is the nonqualified stock option. Stock options are easy incentive tools because they are nondilutive to earnings in the period in which they are issued, and they therefore appear free to the company

FIGURE 3-8

Operating Profit of Dollar General vs. 25th, 50th, and 75th
Percentile of Peer Group

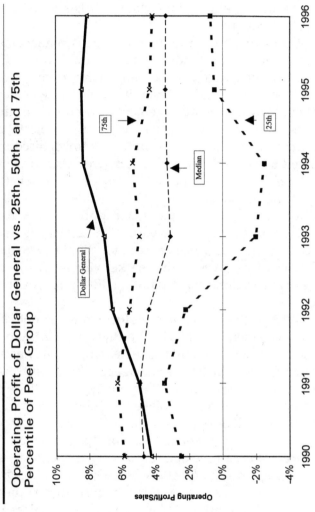

as a means of compensation. They are also tax deductible to the company when they are exercised. Incentives have the very strong effect of focusing management's attention, time, and energy.

Unfortunately, option grants focus management on performance, expectations, and discount rates. Clearly, owners want managers focused on improving the company's performance. However, it is not clear whether owners benefit by having management focused on the other two factors. Management may or may not be able to control expectations, and they have limited control of discount rates (limited to the difference, if any, between the discount rate for the individual company and the overall market).

If the market goes up, a rising tide carries all ships; the stock price of the company will appreciate, and management will receive a nice reward. Figure 3–9 illustrates the percentage of stock price changes for IBM in 1996 that were influenced by moves in the market versus IBM itself. The calculation is done by separating IBM's return from the market's return.

What if the company's performance has not changed but management has received a reward because the stock market price level overall has increased, possibly as a result of lower interest rates? The manager has been paid. But is the pay really for performance? Possibly not. If you look closely at companies that have achieved excellent performance for their shareholders, over time you will see that many of them emphasize relative versus absolute performance. Transamerica is an example of a company that does so by setting stock price appreciation goals before options are granted.

In Transamerica's case, the performance is measured relative to the market. Other companies measure performance relative to their industries and their peers. Relative performance is one of many ways to achieve pay for performance that is truly tied to the performance of the company relative to its peers.

FIGURE   3–9

Percentage of IBM Return Attributable to S&P 500

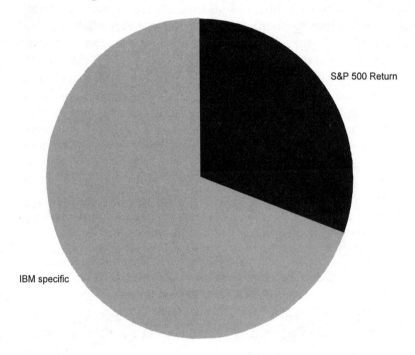

S&P 500 Return

IBM specific

Focus Management on the Business Strategy

Truly excellent companies—the ones that consistently beat the averages and deliver value creation to their sharehold-ers—concentrate on their business strategies. Companies such as Coca-Cola, Wells Fargo, and Mattel focus manage-ment on the key elements of their business strategies. They believe in using performance measures that capture the results of their business strategy, and they pay management for performance above their peers. But they also take the

next step of focusing management by linking performance
to the business strategy (see Table 3–1).

It is this last step of building the bridge between strategy and management decisions that separates the truly innovative companies from the pack and gets the company
aligned to create value. This last step is more difficult to
assess than the previous two because a company is not
required in any disclosure to investors to explain how well
they focus on their business strategy. But you can discern
the company's focus on their business strategy if you carefully read what management writes about performance and
if you listen to what the CEO and line managers say about
their business. There are two tests you can use to see if
management is focused on their strategy: (1) Can management articulate their strategy? and (2) Are they describing
a business strategy or a financial results strategy?

Can Management Articulate
their Strategy?

Many CEOs will say the company's strategy is to grow
earnings at 15 percent per year, deliver a return on equity

T A B L E   3–1

Business Strategies at Coca-Cola, Wells Fargo,
and Mattel

Company	Key Strategies		
Coca-Cola	■ Promote brand awareness	■ Growth	■ Global expansion
Wells Fargo	■ Successful acquisitions	■ New customer acquisition	■ Fee-based income
Mattel	■ Leverage time-tested brands	■ Global growth	

of 20 percent, or some other set of financial goals. This may be a statement of financial objectives, but it is not a strategy. No business can have a strategy solely based on financial outcomes, nor can a company have a strategy without considering financial objectives.

Let me illustrate the first point. Say I'm going to fly from New York to London and that my strategy is to arrive in London by 8 a.m tomorrow. What have I told you? I've told you where I am, where I'm going, and when I hope to arrive, but I've left out the most important ingredient. I have said nothing about how I am going to get to London. Am I going on the Concorde? Is the flight nonstop? Do I plan on flying business class so I can work across the Atlantic? Which airline did I choose?

This is a simple example but one that points out the difference between managing by results and managing by strategy. The CEO who articulates a strategy in terms of a financial outcome has told us that he does not know what his strategy is, that he cannot articulate it, or that he does not want to articulate it. At the same time, one who fails to tell us what financial outcome follows from the strategy has us buying an activity with no clear understanding of the results.

Business Strategy or Financial Results?

To understand how focused management is on the business strategy, the CEO asks the following questions about it: "Is it clear? Does it make sense? Is it expressed in terms of what the company is going to do? How is it going to be done? What will come out of it?"

Table 3–2 illustrates the difference between explaining the relationship between business strategy and financial results by quoting from the 1995 annual reports of Dollar General and Waste Management. What a difference! In the case of Dollar General, you get a very clear picture of the strategy as opposed to Waste Management where the strat-

T A B L E   3-2

Quotes from Dollar General and Waste
Management Annual Reports

Company	Key Strategies
Dollar General	■ Continue to simplify ■ Customer-driven distributor
Waste Management	■ Improve returns on capital ■ Generate/increase owners' cash flow

egy appears to be "get results"—but how the results will be
achieved is a mystery and the business strategy is not clear.

Dollar General talks about their business strategy,
while Waste Management talks about financial results. The
difference is that Dollar General is talking about what they
are going to do to create value, while Waste Management
is talking about what the results will look like if they accomplish what they plan to do.

Sustained value is the ability of a company to earn
higher returns for the shareholders than the competition.
Sustained value can be used as a process for companies
that are anxious to improve their returns to shareholders. By
placing the pieces of the sustained-value equation together,
management can install a value-creation capability in the
organization.

ITS NOT JUST THE SHAREHOLDERS
WHO BENEFIT

Most of the current discussion about value is centered on
value created for the shareholders, but other stakeholders are
involved as well. In the United Kingdom, where the sensitiv-
ity to other stakeholders is politically more apparent than in
the United States, the debate rages about whether the greedy

shareholders are taking money from other stakeholders. Other stakeholders include managers, customers, employees, suppliers, and the communities where the companies are located. In some countries in Western Europe, stakeholders would include the government and trade unions as well.

The common wisdom is that when shareholders win, employees lose. There are cases where shareholders have benefited at the expense of employees where the value created has come as a result of lost jobs sacrificed on the altar of reengineering and downsizing. However, in many companies the reverse is true: Employees have benefited along with the shareholders in the value created. Recently in the United Kingdom, my colleagues at SCA Consulting in London looked into the relationship between shareholders and other stakeholders and found that when shareholders benefit, as measured by total shareholder return (TSR), so do the other stakeholders. This is shown in Figure 3–10 by the relative ranking of companies for the benefits they provide to other stakeholders.[3]

The evidence tells us that managing for value benefits the shareholders, management, employees, customers, suppliers, and the company's competitive position. Seeing the difference in shareholder returns, it is clear how shareholders benefit from value management because when the share price goes up so does their net worth. In a company managed for value, the shareholders will receive excellent returns from their investments, and the shareholders will be more likely to invest additional funds, which will increase management's access to capital for future projects and business-development opportunities.

Managing for value will create direct and indirect benefits for management. The direct benefit for management is greater compensation from the increased value of their stock options. The benefits of improved decision making also extend to management in the form of incentive compensation. Management is compensated for providing returns

FIGURE 3-10

Relationship Between Shareholder and Stakeholder Companies in the United Kingdom

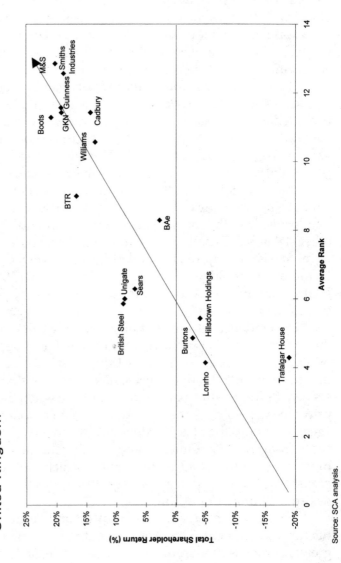

Source: SCA analysis.

to the shareholders. This compensation may take different forms (cash, stock, options, and so on), but improved performance results in improved pay opportunities for management.

Employees gain greater job security from the stronger competitive and economic position of the company. Employees in the company managed for value have greater opportunities for advancement, more growth opportunities, higher wages, and in many cases the opportunity to share in the gains or profits through profit-sharing programs, stock ownership programs, and other financial incentives.

Customers benefit from improved products and services because the greater the value the company creates, the more resources the company can devote to innovation and product development. Customers are likely to see better products and services from the well-run company making decisions for value because the company's resources are better used and dedicated to satisfying customers. This extends to support and service as well. The healthy value-based company is much better able to support and service its product line than the troubled company that is unclear on its strategy.

The portion of the value received by the different constituents varies from company to company and industry to industry, as does the relative importance of the contributors to value. The message, however, is consistent: Value creation benefits many constituents in the company in addition to the shareholders.

CHAPTER 4

Investor Expectations and Strategy

Investors invest capital with the expectation of receiving a return on their investment. Management has the task of earning the return demanded by those investors. But how large a return does management have to earn to satisfy investors? Getting the right answer to this question has high stakes attached to it. If management underdelivers relative to investor expectations, the stock will sell off; if management habitually fails to meet investors' expectations, there may be a new management team.

It is essential that management understands investors' cost of capital and therefore their expectations. In this way, management will be able to match its strategy to those expectations or manage the expectations to align with the strategy. Management's job is to maximize value. To do this job, management must accept and invest in projects with positive returns (good growth) and reject projects with negative returns (bad growth).

Unfortunately, not enough work is done in most companies to understand the investors' expectations. A great deal of emphasis is given to managing *earnings-per-share* in the belief that investors focus only on consistency. But the truth is that investors are looking for something a little more in-depth than just earnings. Investors also want to see the company earn adequate levels of return on capital and the investments the company has made. Investors expect to see that management has a strategy that will continue to produce returns in both the short and long term. Anything less will not satisfy the owners. Would it satisfy you?

First we're going to examine what drives investor expectations and discuss how to measure those expectations. We will then examine how to determine if the company's strategy will deliver enough value to meet the investors' expectations.

WHAT RETURNS ARE INVESTORS LOOKING FOR?

There is no single perspective that defines investor expectations. To determine them, we must gather data to support multiple points-of-view and construct a composite of expectations. The data sources include the following:

- Historical market returns.
- Historical peer and company returns.
- Macroeconomic data.
- Industry and economic forecasts.

The starting place for our composite is the stock market, which provides daily information about investors' expectations for returns. The past is not a perfect predictor of the future, but it provides the starting point for thinking about investor expectations. We will start by choosing a large representative sample of companies, the Standard and Poor's 400 Industrial Average. We can then look at the S&P 400 Industrials over the last 10 years to see what returns the average generated. Figure 4–1 shows the value of $100 in-

FIGURE 4-1

Value of $100 Invested in S&P Industrials (Median)

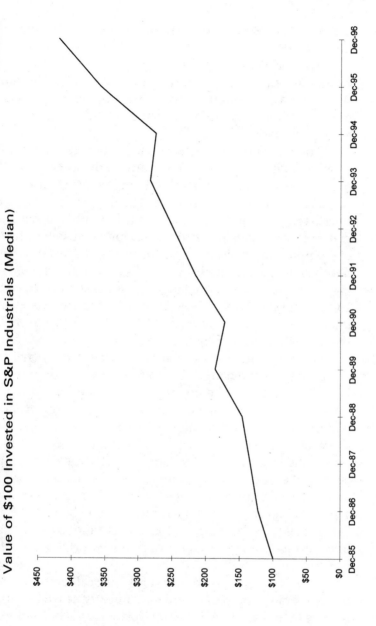

vested in the S&P 400 Industrials for the period from 1986 through 1996.

The S&P 400 is only one of many indices you can use. Others are the S&P 500 and Value Line 1400. The index should be large enough to capture the value-creating performance of a large sample and should be representative of the broad market.

The S&P 400 data contains information about the value creation that results from company and industry performance as well as from macroeconomic factors such as interest rates and tax-policy changes. The movement of interest rates has a profound influence on the level of value creation in the stock market; to appropriately judge the value created by company and industry performance, we need to back out the changes in interest rates. We can adjust the data in Figure 4–1 to back out changes in interest rates over the 10-year period. This is done by calculating the changes in interest rates and removing that percentage return from the value created by the S&P 400. Figure 4–2 shows the annual returns of the S&P 400 Industrials without the benefit or detriment of any changes in interest rates.

The reason for removing interest-rate changes from the historical data is that doing so gives us a more accurate picture of future expectations. This is a clearer picture of the value created by management decisions because it removes the largest macroeconomic change from the picture, leaving the industry and company performance.

When we filter the data for changes in interest rates, we see in Figure 4–2 that the returns earned by the S&P 400 Industrials become more stable across time. By removing interest-rate changes from the data, we reduce the volatility of the index.

The next step is to examine the historical returns earned by comparable companies and the company's own historical returns to investors. When combined with the current market prices, the cost of capital, and interest rates, these three

FIGURE 4-2

S&P Median Return (Ex. Interest Rates, 3-Year Average)

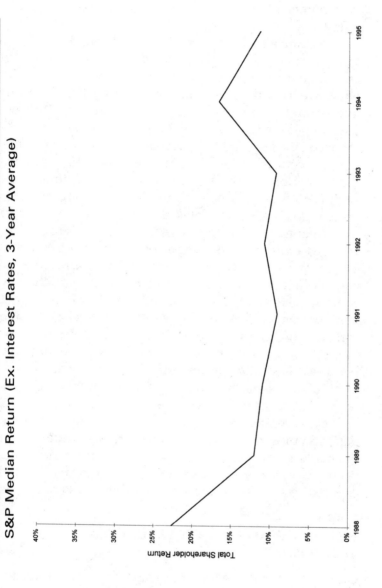

data points allow us to isolate the investors' expectations today.

We can use a simple example here to highlight how historical market, peer, and company data can be integrated into an understanding of investor expectations. The company, which we'll call the Yellow Paper Company, has over the last five years delivered a total shareholder return (TSR) of 12 percent per year to investors. This compares with a median return on the S&P 400 of 13 percent and a median return for the peer companies of 13 percent as well. This company is capable of outperforming the market but historically has slightly underperformed the market over long periods of time. Yellow Paper calculates its cost of equity at 12 percent.

Taking these factors together, a pretty clear picture emerges about investors' expectations for value creation at Yellow Paper: The investors are expecting a return in the neighborhood of 12 to 13 percent. Some of that return will come in the form of dividends. Today Yellow Paper is yielding 3 percent, so we can allocate the 13 percent return to a combination of dividends at 3 percent and the remainder in the form of stock price appreciation of 9 to 10 percent per year. Basically, the investors are saying they expect more of the same returns. Their expectations are in line with the returns they have received in the past.

Most companies are not as easy to analyze as Yellow Paper. Typically, peers have returns that are different from the market, or the company's returns are different from the peers or the market. In these cases, determining the investors' expectations is more difficult than for Yellow Paper.

SO YOU WANT TO OUTPERFORM THE MARKET?

Outperforming the market means beating the market average. Management wants to outperform the market. If we look back at Figure 4–1, we can see what it took to beat the market in each of the last 10 years. We can also look at the data over the entire period and notice that from 1985 through 1996 the S&P 400 Index increased by 271 percent. This represents a compound annual growth in value of 12.7 percent. In addition, we can determine the degree to which companies have outperformed the market by adding to Figure 4–1 information about the 66th, 75th, and 90th percentiles of market performance over the same 10-year period. Figure 4–3 contains this information.

The information in Figure 4–3 still contains the macroeconomic data, so if we want to use the information for investor expectations going forward, we want to filter out the changes in interest rates using the same process we used for the S&P 400 average. When we do this, we get the information in Figure 4–4, which shows the premium over the market you have to earn to be in the 66th, 75th, or 90th percentile in any given year. This is, of course, different from being in the 66th, 75th, or 90th percentile for all the years. If we calculate the return premium above the market to achieve the 66th, 75th, and 90th percentiles for the last full 10-year period, we find that 66th percentile performance translates to a 9-point spread above the market, 75th percentile to a 15-point spread, and 90th percentile to a 30-point spread above the S&P 400 average.

We can compare some of the better-known companies to their value created relative to the S&P 400, as seen in Table 4–1.

How difficult is it to outperform the market in a single period or consistently over time? To answer this question, we need to turn to probability theory, which tells us something about how we need to think about setting targets for future value creation.

Probability theory tells us that in any given year 50 percent of the companies in an average will outperform the average, and in any given two years 25 percent of the companies are likely to outperform an average for each of

FIGURE 4-3

Value of $100 Invested in S&P Industrials

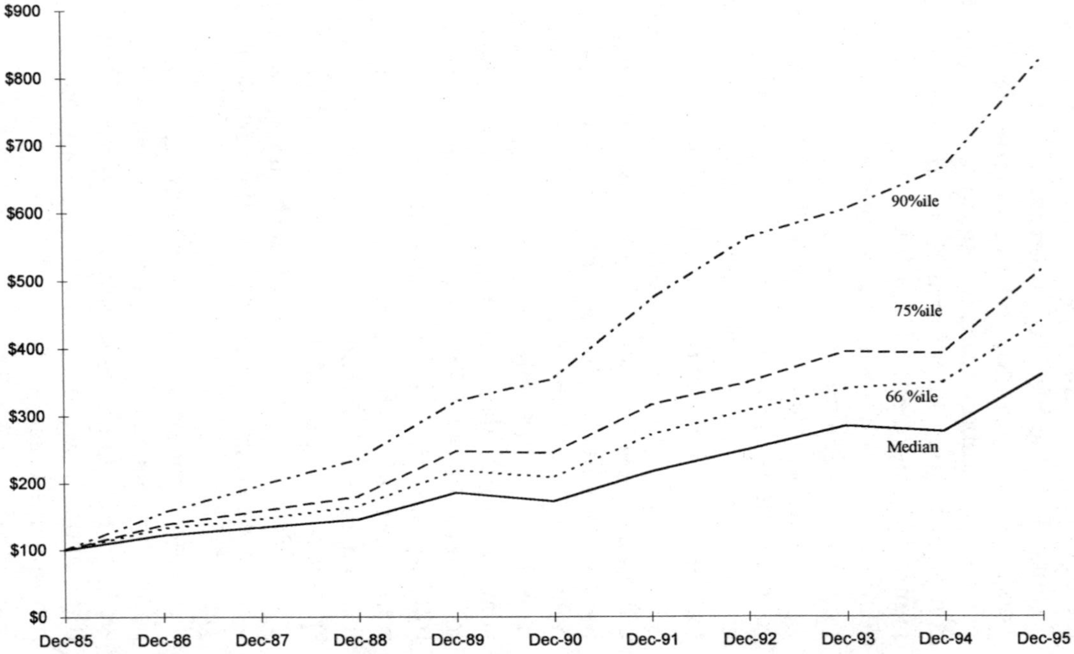

FIGURE 4–4

Premium Over S&P (Ex. Interest Rates, 3-Year Average)

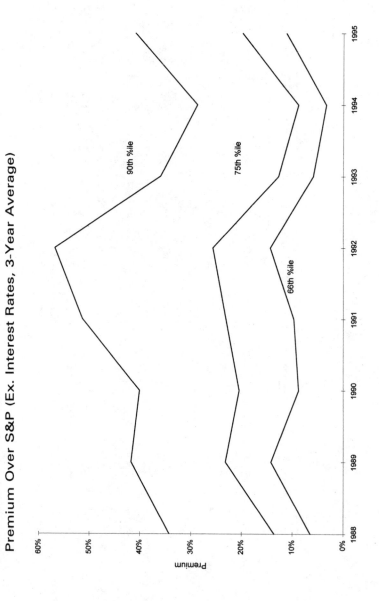

T A B L E 4–1

Percentile Ranks for Each Time Period for Each Company Compared to S&P Industrials

	1986	1987	1988	1989	1990	1991	1992	1993	1994	1995
3M	78%	70%	42%	1%	6%	58%	99%	93%	99%	96%
Coca-Cola	75%	42%	68%	95%	87%	86%	40%	46%	80%	75%
Colgate	62%	33%	71%	61%	84%	54%	60%	59%	55%	31%
Disney	89%	81%	46%	93%	43%	30%	91%	28%	65%	53%
General Electric	49%	46%	30%	73%	46%	55%	56%	73%	45%	73%
General Motors	23%	36%	88%	29%	40%	8%	56%	94%	10%	52%
IBM	6%	34%	42%	5%	90%	7%	1%	58%	92%	48%
Intel	4%	96%	12%	71%	78%	45%	96%	88%	52%	96%
Johnson & Johnson	59%	62%	56%	66%	88%	78%	13%	17%	88%	88%
Kodak	78%	56%	18%	17%	70%	38%	11%	88%	65%	72%
Merck	97%	78%	47%	60%	84%	91%	7%	10%	76%	95%
Motorola	15%	84%	8%	63%	42%	44%	93%	95%	90%	13%
Texas Instruments	39%	86%	2%	11%	73%	6%	91%	84%	84%	68%

those two years (.5 × .5 = .25). Table 4–2 reproduces the theory for us to see just how difficult it is to outperform the market in successive years.

Now let's return to reality and compare the theory with what actually happened. When we take the theory and apply it to the S&P 400, we expect 50 companies to outperform the average in three consecutive years. In fact, for the period 1993–1995, 46 did outperform. Figure 4–5 reproduces the results of research into how closely the theory matches what actually happened for 1986–1995. As you can see, the theory does a pretty good job. This is good news for management because it helps establish the degrees of difficulty for exceeding investor expectations.

This analysis supports the idea that markets in aggregate are efficient because the number of companies that actually outperform is very close to the theoretical results. This suggests we can expect to outperform and that undervalued and overvalued companies balance each other out.

WHAT LEVEL OF RISK?

What level of risk are investors willing to accept in your company's stock? The answer to this question is simultaneously complex and simple. It is complex because investors have their own beliefs about risk, which they have assessed implicitly or explicitly in setting a value on the company's stock. The simple answer is that the return the investors expect to earn is risk-adjusted. This means the issue of risk for our purposes of assessing investors' expectations for returns is somewhat of a nonissue; whatever risk they expect or have assessed is already included in the stock price at the starting time. For example, if an investor believes the risk of IBM delivering a 10 percent return is greater as a function of the uncertainty of the mainframe market, increased competition, or a variety of other reasons, the investor has already included that judgment in the value he or

T A B L E 4–2

Table of Probability Theory on Exceeding Market Expectations

Percentile	Number of Consecutive Years									
	1	2	3	4	5	6	7	8	9	10
50th	50.00	25.00	12.50	6.25	3.13	1.56	0.78	0.39	0.20	0.10

FIGURE 4-5

S&P Industrial Companies Exceeding the S&P Median Return Three Years in a Row

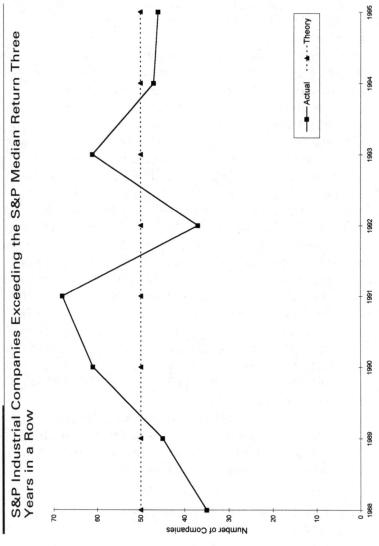

she has established for the stock by establishing a lower value to account for the perceived risk. The investor's judgments about risk, industry cyclicality, and consistency of meeting prior expectations are already baked into today's stock price. We can look at the returns to be earned in the future as the risk-adjusted returns because the investor has already done all the risk-assessment work for us.

Let's take the information we have accumulated so far and set a target based on investor expectations for IBM. If IBM wants to deliver a 66th percentile return to investors, we can add 9 percent to the expected return for the market and come up with a target for IBM's return to investors. The targeted return can then be translated into a stock price target by subtracting IBM's dividend yield from the return to investors and increasing the value of the stock by the remaining percentage return yearly. If IBM wanted a 66th percentile return, which we translated into an 18 percent return to investors by adding the 9 percent to the anticipated market return of 9 percent, we then subtract IBM's dividend yield of 2 percent resulting in a stock price appreciation target of 16 percent. If we apply the stock price appreciation target to the 1996 year-end stock price of $151.50 and forecast the stock price in five years, we anticipate a target stock price of $279 [obtained by $151.50 x $(1.16)^5 = \$279.12$]. Figure 4–6 illustrates the calculation.

There are many subtleties to the targeting process, but when you have calculated a price appreciation target for the stock price, the next question becomes whether or not the strategy you have gets you to your target.

WILL YOUR STRATEGY MEET EXPECTATIONS?

Do you know how much value your company's strategy will create? What is the strategy's objective? Is the level of planned value creation enough to satisfy investors? Will

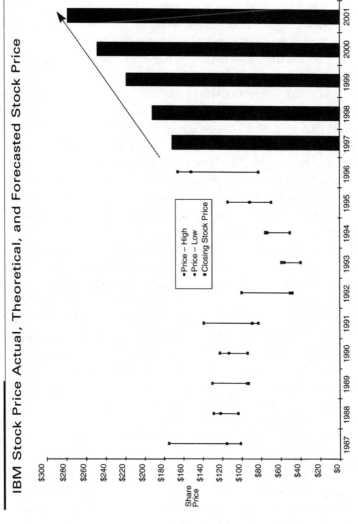

FIGURE 4-6

IBM Stock Price Actual, Theoretical, and Forecasted Stock Price

the strategy satisfy investors? Companies that can answer these questions have a clearer road map to meeting investor expectations and creating value. Figure 4–7 depicts stock prices for IBM. You know what value IBM created, but do you know how much value they will create?

Knowing how much value you plan to create is better than not knowing. Management should always prefer to know whether or not the plan they have will meet investors' expectations. There are, of course, many business issues that can and will come up over the plan period that you can't foresee as you develop the plan. These will need to be addressed and factored into the plan as they arise. You can assess whether your strategy will meet expectations and adjust the strategy and business plan if they fall short. The cost of doing this is far less than the cost of failing to meet investors' expectations.

Knowing the value of the strategic plan helps to answer the questions, "Are we going to meet our investors' expectations?" and "Is the strategy good enough?" A logical starting place is to determine investors' expectations. The difficulty is that companies find it harder and harder to perform higher than expectations, and yet investors continue to require returns, so it becomes very important to management and investors whether or not your strategy gets you to investors' expectations. Two questions must be answered: (1) Does the strategy meet expectations? and (2) How achievable is the strategy?

It may seem obvious that a strategic plan should meet investor expectations. However, many plans do not, and investors find themselves disappointed when the company fails to deliver the returns investors expected. When this happens, the stock drops, wealth is destroyed, and management finds themselves with stock options that are under water and sometimes with less-than-buoyant job security. Very few companies go through the process of valuing their strategic plan. Yet, unless you know the value

IBM Stock Price—High, Low, and Close

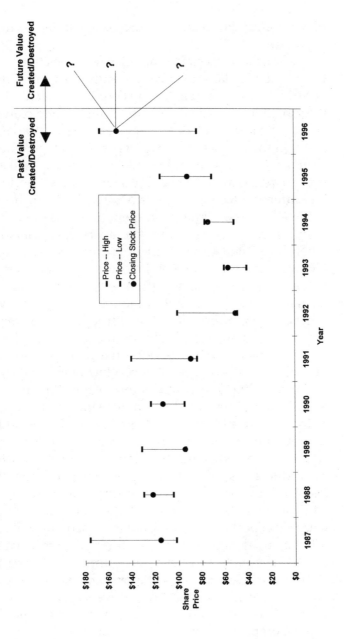

of your strategic plan, you are flying blind in uncertain weather.

A primary reason companies have hesitated to value their strategic plans is concern over the cost and complexity of hiring investment bankers to conduct the valuations. But it is possible to value the company's strategic plan using a simpler and less-costly technique. Typically, companies talk about improving financial results or achieving higher levels of financial performance. How much value will the improved performance create? Using financial performance measurement techniques, it is possible to define how much value a business strategy or alternative business strategies will create. Figure 4–8 illustrates a strategic plan valuation when forecasted forward in time and related to the high and low historical range of the company's stock price. This value is not the same as current price because the market does not have the same information as the plan. Even if it did have the information, the market might or might not believe in management's ability to execute the plan.

It is also possible to value the parts of the company by looking at the divisions' or product lines' strategic plans and measuring their contribution to value creation. Figure 4–9 illustrates how a valuation of a strategic plan based on a divisional buildup to stock price contributes additional information. In this case, the divisions submit their plans, which are valued using the financial plans of the divisions or product lines. Of course, no plan is perfect or omniscient, and the actual events that occur over the operating period will vary from the plan. Valuing the plan is meant to tell us what we expect will happen, not what actually will happen. What actually happens will be different from what we expected. The purpose, then, is to compare our expectations relative to investors' expectations and to make sure the differences can be explained and resolved.

Let's return to the story of our friends at the Yellow Paper Company. Yellow Paper's plan calls for a stock price

FIGURE 4-8

Strategic Plan's Predicted Stock Price (Year 2000)

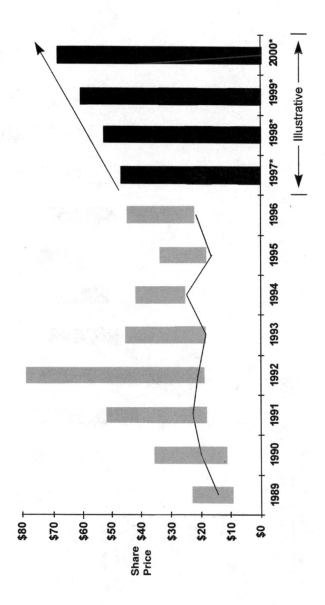

FIGURE 4-9

Divisional Buildup

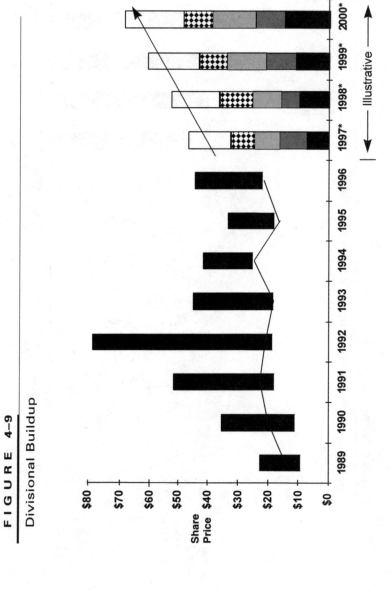

of $19 per share. Understanding how far short of expectations the plan falls helps the company understand how much improvement in the plan is needed.

Valuing the plan addresses the first question of strategy by helping us to understand how much value the plans we have will create and how good a job we are doing of meeting investor expectations. The next question concerns the achievability of the plan. To understand achievability, we need to review the assumptions in the strategic plan. Quite often, strategic plans are forecasts showing ever-improving results not well-grounded in reality. These plans showing improving results are often referred to as "hockey stick" forecasts and are usually extrapolated from next year's budget or last year's performance. They are usually based on simplistic assumptions about future growth or profitability that fail to account for real-world conditions or analyze competitive and market position and capabilities. Understanding what assumptions went into the creation of the plan can be very helpful. The assumptions can then be pressure tested to determine how confident management is in its ability to achieve the strategic plan.

Figure 4–10 illustrates some of the techniques management can use to pressure test the strategic plan. When you pressure test, you are interested in knowing how the assumptions in the plan stack up relative to other possibilities, competitors' performance, and the past performance of the company as well as what type of investment is required to achieve the plan.

Is the degree of difficulty in the plan high or low? Is it reasonable to expect that the management team can execute the strategic plan and get the desired results? How difficult is it to achieve the plan? Pressure testing the plan reveals the answers to these questions and helps management judge whether or not the plan is reasonable. There is danger in convincing investors you can execute a plan when the plan is a stretch and has a high likelihood of failure.

F I G U R E 4–10

Potential Methods for Pressure Testing Targets

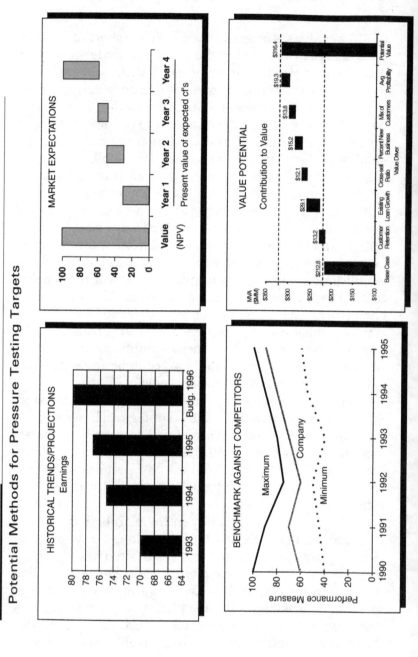

Two issues can emerge from the analysis of likelihood of success. The first identifies when the plan meets investors' expectations but is not likely to be achievable. This is usually the case in "hockey stick" type plans where the assumptions do not stand up under a pressure testing of the business logic. The second identifies when the plan is achievable and appears reasonable under pressure testing but fails to meet the investors' expectations for returns. These issues suggest the plan needs to be rethought. When the strategic plan calls for creating the level of value desired by investors, and the quality of the assumptions in the plan is understood, management is much better equipped to execute the plan and meet investors' expectations.

For an illustration of how the strategies of two companies exceeded, met, or fell short of investor expectations, we can look at Wal-Mart and Kmart. These two companies in the same industry chose very different strategies and achieved very different results.

In 1980, Wal-Mart was a $1.6 billion company with 276 stores. Kmart was a $14.1 billion company with 1,885 stores. Wal-Mart was earning a return of 7.2 percent, while Kmart was earning 5.5 percent. What happened over the next 10 years became a business legend. By 1990, every dollar that had been invested in Wal-Mart in 1980 was worth $33.50, while every dollar invested in Kmart was worth only $3.60.

The reasons for the results are even more interesting than the results themselves. In 1980, Kmart held the dominant position in discount retailing with substantial economies of scale in their operations. Wal-Mart knew they needed to do things differently if they were going to take business away from Kmart. The overall discount retail industry was not growing that rapidly in 1980. If Wal-Mart wanted to create value for their shareholders, they had to grow their number of stores, improve the profitability of the business, or both. Growth meant taking business away from others. If Wal-Mart was going to create value, they could not just compete with Kmart head-to-head.

In the 10 years following 1980, Wal-Mart's focus on customer satisfaction and pulling costs out of their business led to such innovative ideas as cross-docking, which allowed fewer square feet per store and lower inventory levels. Each company's returns over the 10 years are illustrated in Figure 4–11(a). The value created for investors is shown in Figure 4–11(b). At the beginning of 1980, Kmart had a strong economy-of-scale advantage over Wal-Mart because of sheer size as shown in Figure 4–11(c). This should have translated into a cost advantage, higher returns, and greater value creation.

Unfortunately, Kmart frittered away their advantage through a poor understanding of their targeted customer base, changing demographics, and deteriorating stores. In just 10 short years, Kmart lost the scale advantage they had enjoyed for decades and ceded the position as leading discount retailer to Wal-Mart. Wal-Mart realized early on they would need to compete differently than Kmart. There were other ways to compete and create value that built on Wal-Mart's strengths. By focusing on these strengths and competing differently, Wal-Mart increased their sales per store, as shown in Figure 4–11(d). In the end, Wal-Mart met or exceeded investors' expectations, while Kmart disappointed investors.

Companies make decisions about how they compete on an ongoing basis. In making these decisions, managers make trade-offs in the uses of expense and capital dollars to generate revenue opportunities. The opportunities are usually defined by the resources committed to achieving them. In the process of allocating the resources, management makes decisions that involve compromising revenue opportunity.

It is difficult to get to a destination unless you know the destination before you set out on your trip. Most people

F I G U R E   4–11

(a) Return on Sales Kmart and Wal-Mart.

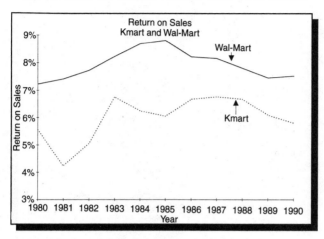

(b) Value of $100 Invested in Kmart vs. Wal-Mart.

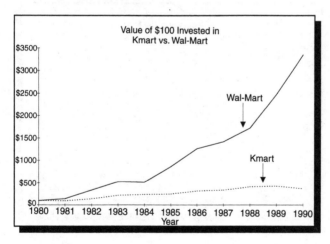

F I G U R E   4–11 (Continued)

(c) Net Sales: Kmart and Wal-Mart.

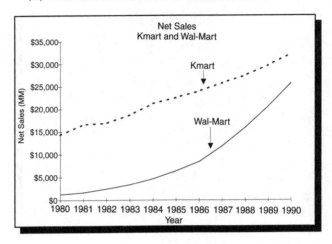

(d) Sales per Store: Kmart and Wal-Mart.

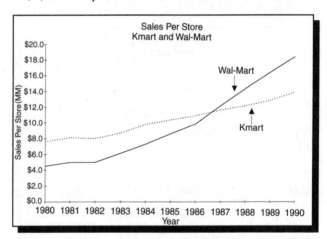

also measure their rate of progress toward the destination. However, when it comes to strategy, many companies turn a deaf ear to measuring their performance against the strategy. Measuring progress is not that difficult, so why doesn't management want to measure it? One reason is the difficulty in valuing the strategy. However, knowing whether or not you are planning to meet investors' expectations is an important, if not vital, piece of management information.

When we talk about the intersection of value creation and business strategy, we are talking about value management. In the next chapter, we will discuss what value management is and how to manage for value.

What is Value Management?

Managing for value is nothing new. Excellent companies, particularly companies where the founder is the CEO, have used value-based decision-making concepts for centuries. Yet, today few companies are realizing the maximum value they could create.

In this chapter, we will define what it means to manage for value and explain how managing for value can play an important role in investment and operating decisions. We will discuss how a focus on value can help management make trade-offs between different opportunities and conflicting priorities. We will describe how creating value generates competitive advantage for the company and how the competitive advantage allows the company to create even more value for investors. Surprisingly, managing for value has only been adopted in a small number of companies. In Chapter 10, we will discuss the reasons for the lack of success and look at companies like Quaker Oats that have tried value management and failed.

Value management is a way of focusing managers on the company's strategy, to achieve better alignment, and create value. Managing for value means using the right combination of capital and other resources to generate cash flow from the business. Value management is not an event that occurs once a year but is an ongoing process of investing and operating decision making that includes a focus on value creation.

Cash flow is generated by wisely investing and operating the business. Each investing or operating decision has the opportunity to create value. The quality of the decision making contributes to the value created. Decision making has three elements: objectives, alternatives, and information. Introducing a focus on value into each decision-making element helps improve the quality of the decision and creates value.

Managing for value is a mind-set focused on creating value built on a foundation of good decisions that are aligned between the four key management processes. Managing for value focuses managers and provides insights into the trade-offs that managers are implicitly making, generating a broader set of alternatives, and improving the information used to make decisions. Managers face conflicts in making decisions, including different objectives and time horizons, uncertainty, limited resources, and multiple priorities. These conflicts are what lead to a dilution of focus. Managing for value means imposing on existing businesses the same type of discipline applied to new project approval.

Value management can be used as a tool in decision making both at the corporate center and in operations. Value-managed companies focus on value-oriented decision making in the four key management processes of planning, budgeting, compensation, and management reporting. Together, when focused on value, these key management processes reinforce the value mind-set. Figure 5–1 illustrates how the key management processes can reinforce the key stages of value-based thinking.

F I G U R E 5–1

Relationship of Management Processes to Value-Based Thinking

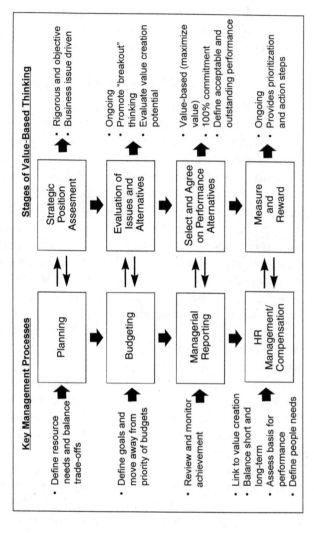

Key Management Processes

- Define resource needs and balance trade-offs
- Define goals and move away from priority of budgets
- Review and monitor achievement
- Link to value creation
- Balance short and long-term
- Assess basis for performance
- Define people needs

Planning ⇄ **Strategic Position Assesment**

Budgeting ⇄ **Evaluation of Issues and Alternatives**

Managerial Reporting ⇄ **Select and Agree on Performance Alternatives**

HR Management/ Compensation ⇄ **Measure and Reward**

Stages of Value-Based Thinking

- Rigorous and objective
- Business issue driven

- Ongoing
- Promote "breakout" thinking
- Evaluate value creation potential

- Value-based (maximize value)
- 100% commitment
- Define acceptable and outstanding performance

- Ongoing
- Provides prioritization and action steps

103

VALUE-BASED DECISION MAKING

The three elements of decision making are: objectives, alternatives, and information. Each of these elements contributes to the focus on value.

Objectives

In theory, the objective of any decision is to create value, but in real life, things are often more complex. Often, an organization has conflicting objectives that require managers to make trade-offs.

A simple example of conflicting objectives can be illustrated in the decision to purchase a new machine that will reduce costs. Let's say that the new machine will not only reduce costs, but because the new machine is more automated, it will also require fewer people to operate it. So, the investment makes sense. However, the company is facing conflicting objectives of lower costs versus lower employee morale because, although buying the machine will reduce costs, it also involves employee layoffs.

This is a simple example. The more complex the business, the greater the number of conflicts between objectives in different parts of the organization. One of the most common conflicts occurs between sales and manufacturing functions where sales makes promises to the customers and manufacturing must deliver on the promises while balancing other considerations, such as inventory levels, run times, and machine downtime.

As the complexity of the company increases, so do the number of conflicts. Managers must make trade-offs between objectives, which is difficult to do without a single, overriding objective that provides guidance in making the trade-offs. Managing for value provides the weighing scale to help managers balance different considerations, make trade-offs, and come to decisions that maximize value for the organization.

Alternatives

Often, the alternatives examined in the decision-making process are too narrowly focused on the existing way of doing business. Managing for value can introduce the discipline of expanding the decision making to encompass a broader range of alternatives. For example, consider a company that typically leases capital equipment such as delivery trucks. The company is in the process of deciding whether or not to lease additional equipment for expansion. Currently, 25 percent of the company's equipment is leased, while its competitors lease only 5 percent. Why the big difference?

A few years back, the company had gone through a financially difficult period; the leasing preference was a vestige of the period when the company experienced difficulty obtaining bank financing. The company's financial condition is now much stronger, but the company continues to lease equipment even though it is more costly to lease than to buy. A focus on value improved the decision making by increasing the number of alternatives under consideration to include purchasing the new trucks with debt financing.

Information

Quality information is the third element of good decision making. Improving the quality of the information will improve the decision making. Decisions are frequently made with imperfect, incomplete, or poor information. In the prior example, managers can improve the quality of information by identifying the equipment required and comparing it with the equipment competitors are using. Managers can also improve the quality of information by examining the returns from the new equipment and comparing those returns to the existing equipment. For one company in the transportation business, we found the returns on the existing equipment were consistently below the projected returns on the new equipment. In probing further, we found that the returns on new equipment contained very optimistic assumptions. This information helped the company examine new capital requests to ensure that the capital requests were based on reasonable business assumptions.

Take the example of a company considering a new plant. Should the company build the plant in a location that provides the best environment for employees, only consider the economic cost of building the plant, or combine both objectives and build the plant where it will be the cheapest to construct and where employees will be happiest working? Although one location may result in higher costs due to higher wages, taxes, and other expenses of operating the business, the other location may have higher costs associated with job turnover and employee morale, which will offset the expected advantages of the first location. For this company, improving the information concerning these issues will lead to a better understanding of the alternatives.

Improving the information used in decision making represents a critical opportunity for management to focus on value. A company we will call Healthco was very successful for many years, but recently its financial results have come under a lot of pressure. Table 5–1 shows the company's return on equity from 1992 to 1995.

Healthco's return on equity (ROE) was very strong for many years. The company was pursuing a geographic expansion strategy that enabled it to acquire regional companies in the same business and then cut costs by eliminating overhead while maintaining the acquired business' revenue level. The company used different organizational entities to operate their different local businesses. In 1995, the company centralized inventory and supplier relationships to reduce costs but failed to build adequate informa-

TABLE 5-1

Healthco Return on Equity

Year	1992	1993	1994	1995
ROE	15%	18%	21%	8%

tion systems to support the combination of centralized and decentralized activities. The result of poor systems integration was a lack of quality information for decision making, which resulted in numerous poor decisions and a marked drop in financial performance. The decline in financial performance as measured by return on equity is shown in Table 5-1.

Quality information is critical for decision making. Companies that have better information can use it to gain insights that will enable them to achieve competitive advantages over their rivals.

THE DECISION-MAKING PROCESS

Management faces decisions with conflicting objectives every day and has to make trade-offs to select the best decisions. Using value as the objective for decision making helps to balance the multiple perspectives and helps managers think through the trade-offs they are being asked to make. Using value as the objective for decision making defines the goal, reduces uncertainty, and encourages managers to think through the ramifications of their decisions.

Many large companies are mired in a cumbersome decision-making process. One example is Apple Computer. At Apple, the lack of value-based decision making hurt the company and its competitive position. Market share, which peaked at 10 percent in 1994, did not achieve sufficient critical mass to sustain the brand. For a period of 10 years, the Macintosh operating system commanded a substantial technical advantage and a perceived ease-of-use advantage over the competing MS-DOS/Windows operating systems. During this time, Apple refused to license the Macintosh operating system. This decision was a key strategic blunder and cost the company dearly in sales and, more importantly, in their installed base of users. Because Macintosh never exceeded 10 percent of the installed base of personal computers, it was by definition a second choice to MS-DOS and later Windows as a platform for software application development.

The consequences of Apple's failure to license its operating system were severe. From 1991 to 1996, Apple's stock price fell from $73 per share to $16 per share. Apple's management destroyed $6.8 billion in shareholder value in the five years from 1991 to 1996. Even this figure obscures the true magnitude of the loss because over the same period the S&P 500 increased shareholder value by an average of 169 percent. Taking this opportunity cost into account, Apple's shareholders lost $126 in value for every $100 invested! Figure 5–2 shows the decline in the value of a $100 investment in Apple made in December 1991.

Apple's objectives lacked clarity during the late 1980s and early 1990s. The poor decision making that led to this value destruction at Apple in the early 1990s was a result of poor information, focus on opinion over fact, and increasing difficulty in making trade-offs. How could trade-offs be made without a clear basis for making them?

How could this happen? Apple was viewed as an American icon of creative capabilities and innovative management. Although innovative on the surface, Apple's management was paralyzed by poor decision making. All Apple managers who were potentially affected by a decision got a vote, so no one could make a decision unless all interested parties agreed, resulting in decision-making paralysis. Prod-

FIGURE 5-2

Value of $100 Invested in Apple Computer

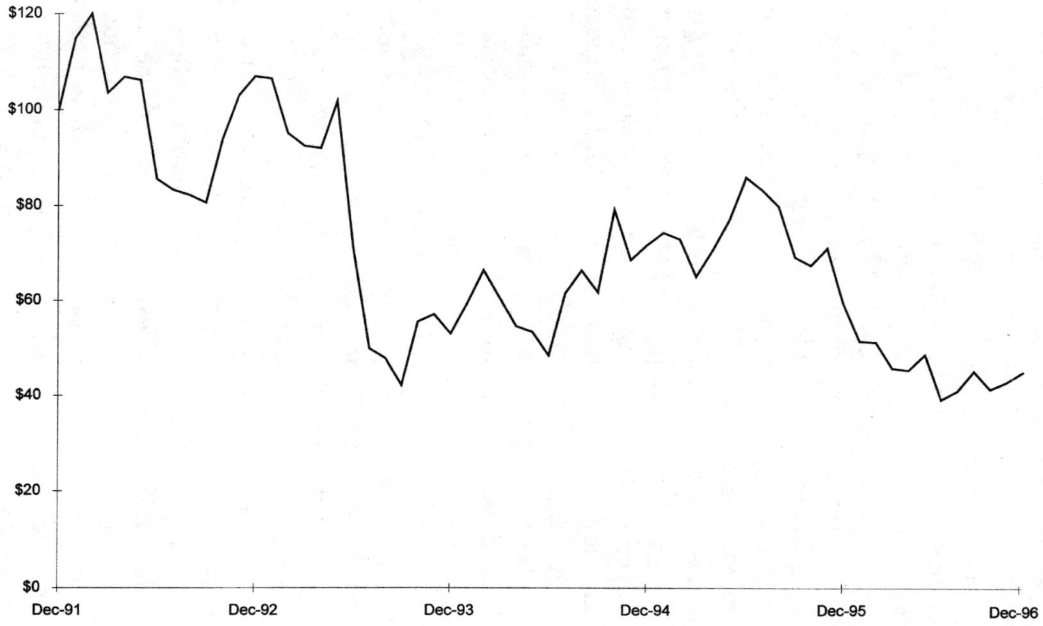

uct development got to vote on marketing and could re-arrange the product introduction schedule at will, while manufacturing could not be done unless marketing agreed to the production plans. This tyranny of pluralism was so cumbersome it lead Michael Spindler, the CEO who followed John Sculley, to personally make most decisions of any importance. Imagine a $10 billion company where the CEO is deciding on expense budget line items in individual departments and making the decisions on production. No matter how good a decision maker Spindler was, there is no way he could single-handedly have the information to make all the consequential decisions in the company.

Another example of Apple's poor decision making involved the hurdle rates the company used for new projects. For a long time, new projects had to earn a 30 percent return to get funded. This meant that projects that did not meet the 30 percent hurdle rate—and very few did—were not funded. Apple was not short on cash; in the late 1980s the company's operations were earning returns on net assets in excess of 22 percent. But rather than invest in projects below the 30 percent return threshold, the company instead accumulated cash and simply put it in the bank. By 1991, Apple had over $1 billion of cash that was earning a relatively paltry 3 percent return after tax.

Different areas of the Apple organization justified decisions in any way they found convenient; there was no single objective by which to evaluate alternatives. There were multiple conflicting priorities, such as ease of use, user experience, consumer marketing, business marketing, product marketing, and many new product ideas (few of which were actually introduced) that sent conflicting signals to management. When these conflicting signals were compounded with the lack of a sound decision-making process, where opinion counted for as much if not more than fact-based information, the result was confusion and organizational paralysis.

Apple is one of the more egregious examples of poor decision making, but they are not alone. In many companies, the decision-making process frequently takes too long and leads to decisions not being made, decisions being deferred, and lost opportunities. Many books have been written about the abilities of fleet-footed organizations to gain competitive advantage at the expense of tortoise-like competitors.

Apple could have avoided the poor decision-making trap had the company developed an orientation to value-based decision making and value-based management processes. Instead, the company failed to develop and implement either disciplined management decision making or the management processes.

Decision making at Apple suffered from conflicting objectives. There was no understanding of the link between decisions and how outcomes might affect value. This absence of a "line-of-sight" that relates decisions to their value impact resulted in numerous poor decisions. Examples include Apple's 1989 price increases that responded to increased memory cost, the proliferation of product families, and the focus on gross margin percentages instead of gross margin dollars. Many of these poor decisions could have been avoided if the decision makers understood the impact of their decisions on value creation.

Why did Apple's stock remain high for as long as it did? Institutional investors were very aware of the problems. Despite the stock price declines experienced after the announcement of every bad decision, Apple's stock continued to defy gravity while optimism triumphed in the face of reality.

PROCESSES SHOULD REINFORCE VALUE-CREATING DECISIONS

Value management is more than just value-based decision making. The decisions must be supported by an environment that encourages value creation, and the decision-

making environment is largely set by four key management processes:

1. Planning.
2. Budgeting.
3. Compensation.
4. Reporting.

Let's take each of these four key management processes
one by one and explore how value management can and
does enrich each activity.

Planning

Planning takes information about the operating and strategic characteristics of the business today and assumptions
about the future, adds knowledge from inside and outside
the company, and converts this information into a plan that
usually includes economic, market, and financial projections. Planning is the process that focuses on strategy; making sure the company's resources are being appropriately
deployed for competitive advantage. A value measure can
then be used to convert the financial projections into information on how much value the plan will create under the
given assumptions. The value measure used in planning
can then be used in other key management processes to
provide consistent signals to decision makers. Figure 5–3
illustrates the link between strategic planning and other
management processes.

A value measure can help management move beyond
a simplistic view of sales growing by "x" percent or earnings
increasing by "y" percent to a deeper more comprehensive
understanding of the trade-offs between improved operating results and growth. The banking industry provides
an example of this, where planning departments traditionally forecasted higher earnings. The full extent of planning
simply targeted selling more credit by selling more loans

FIGURE 5-3

Key Management Processes

to existing corporate customers or finding new customers for existing loan products. For many years, the formula worked just fine, and banks performed well for their shareholders. However, as the structure of financial services started to change in the 1980s and other forms of financing became available to corporations and corporate customers had greater access to liquidity in the public markets, the demand for traditional loans dropped. The result was a squeeze on the profitability of loans. Margins on loans to corporate customers fell from 300 basis points to less than 100.

The pressure on profits in the credit business, which was one of the traditional bastions of bank profitability, was enormous. Banks that responded with more of the same old recipe of selling more credit and selling credit harder watched their profits and shareholder value fall behind that of their peers. The competitive landscape was changing. Smart competitors had awakened to the efficient use of capital and learned how to use it more wisely. Many of the banks that continued to pursue credit as their sole avenue to growth were acquired by competitors who understood and responded to the structural changes occurring in financial services. Table 5–2 lists some of the significant consolidations that occurred in banking from 1990 to 1995.

Using value in their planning process helped some of the surviving institutions see the structural changes occurring in the industry, the influences of these changes on value, the range of competitive alternatives open to them, and how those alternatives compared favorably to the status quo.

Value management does not replace good planning; it augments it. Both are essential ingredients for success.

T A B L E   5–2

Consolidation in Banking from 1990–1995

BankAmerica and Security Pacific
BankAmerica and Continental Bank
Chase Manhattan and Chemical Bank
Corestates Financial and First Pennsylvania
Corestates Financial and Meridian Bancorp
First Chicago and NBD
Fleet Financial and Shawmut National
KeyCorp and Society Corp
U.S. Bancorp and West One Bancorp
U.S. Bancorp and California Bancshares
Wells Fargo and Great American Bank
Wells Fargo and First Interstate

Budgeting

Typically, budgeting is limited to one year and may, but does not necessarily, connect directly to the long-range plan. Budgeting involves the commitment of capital and a focus on near-term operating results. It is in the budgeting process that the operating expenses for the coming year are estimated and the resources are committed.

The budgeting process is concerned with allocating resources, usually capital, to the different product lines or business units. Value measurement plays an important role by placing the different opportunities on a level playing field for comparison of the opportunities.

Resource allocation is often suboptimal because the decisions to make investments are made piecemeal and focus on the incremental investment while giving little consideration to the existing investment. Multiple business units in different businesses each bring their cases forward for increased investment, and corporate management must choose between the competing proposals.

As an example, let's look at a media company with business units in newspapers, television, and publishing. The asset intensity of each business is very different, as is the profitability of the different businesses (see Figure 5–4).

Is a dollar of investment in each of these businesses going to yield an equivalent dollar of value, and if not, what is the difference? Figure 5–5 illustrates the marginal value that shareholders will receive from an investment in one of these businesses over the other.

This implies that if capital is limited, management should prioritize investments based on the value they add for shareholders. The budget uses a value measure in much the same way it is used in planning. The value measure helps management explore, weigh, and balance the trade-offs between capital, revenue, and expenses. One of the

FIGURE 5-4

Media Company Asset Intensity and Profitability

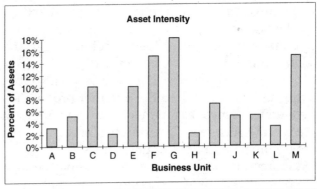

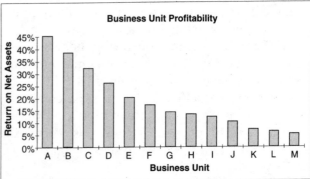

areas where budgeting runs into trouble is when it becomes an advocacy or negotiating process. Quite often, compensation is linked to achieving the budget. This is a recipe for poor budgeting because the outcome is a negotiation process that is designed to keep the budgeted results as easy to achieve as possible. A much better alternative is to uncouple budgeting from compensation.

Marginal Value Per Dollar Invested in the Business Units of a
Media Company

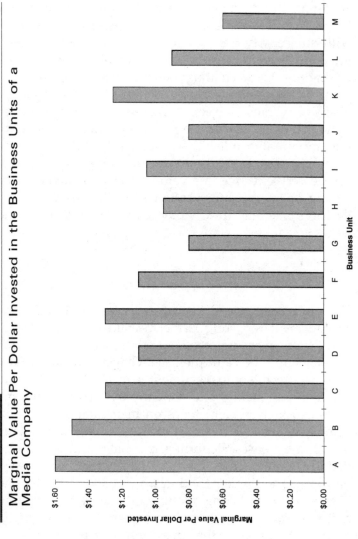

Compensation

Traditionally, compensation has been the financial backwater of the corporation, dominated by measures loaded with subjectivity and discretion that are not necessarily linked to other processes. Today, excellent companies are paying for value-creating performance as an important piece of their compensation strategies. This emphasis on objective versus subjective measures and of informed judgment over "seat-of-the-pants" management is producing important results. Discretion and nonfinancial measures, when properly used to augment objective measures, can be very effective in a value-managed company. Introducing value to compensation turbocharges value-based decision making. In Chapter 8, we will discuss these issues in greater detail.

Reporting

The old truism states, "What gets measured gets done." Management reporting is the measurement of what gets done. Value measures can be used in reporting to reinforce the managing-for-value message. They provide information on how effectively management is using the capital in the business to generate returns. Only by reporting the measures can management focus on managing for value and provide information on the trade-offs between capital, revenue, and expenses. Reporting is usually, but need not be, tied to a single period. Rarely do investment initiatives pay off during the single period in which they are made. There is great value in taking a longer time horizon in planning and integrating this view into budgeting. A longer time horizon also provides the opportunity to report on the progress of investment initiatives.

One of the criticisms leveled against management today condemns management's short-term focus. If a single period's results are being measured, is it really a great surprise that the focus is on the short term? The short-term orientation of many managers leads to short-term decision making at the expense of the long-term value of the business. When properly specified and implemented, value management can provide a longer-term orientation by providing balance between the factors that lead to short-term performance with the longer-term factors necessary for sustained competitive performance.

COMMUNICATION

Communication ties all the processes together and provides management with the opportunity to internally and externally discuss the company's goals. Management must explain how they will measure the company's progress against the goals, how the business strategies deliver value, and what role employees play in value creation. As Figure 5–6 suggests, the focus on managing for value must be included in all four key management processes, or the different processes will send conflicting signals to management.

A clear example of a company that manages value through the four key management processes is Southwest Airlines, which has a 4 percent market share of the U.S. passenger airline market. The company was started in 1971 and until 1991 had less than 2 percent of the U.S. air passenger market. In the three years from 1992 to 1995, Southwest's market share doubled, while the company maintained profitable performance in all quarters, unlike other major carriers. Southwest has a competitive advantage over the other major carriers because its costs are lower. This advantage has led to fierce price competition. But while cost advantage explains some of the competitive advantage Southwest has achieved, it does not explain all of it.

In 1980, another start-up airline entered the U.S. market with a cost advantage: People Express. People had the same

F I G U R E 5–6

Key Management Processes

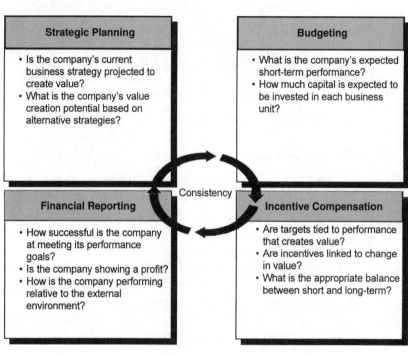

or better cost position than Southwest. In fact, in 1982 People's cost per seat mile was somewhat less than Southwest's. But People is no longer in business, having fallen prey to overexpansion and higher costs. Southwest avoided the same fate by making better decisions. The impact of these decisions is readily apparent when we look at Southwest's returns on operations and returns to shareholders over the last 10 years. Southwest expanded, but unlike People Express where the expansion was swift, Southwest followed a deliberate, incremental expansion strategy, always making sure they could make money before expanding.

Figure 5–7 illustrates Southwest's performance for shareholders over the last 10 years. A $100 investment in Southwest in December 1986 was worth $533 in 1996, while a $100 investment in the average major airline was worth $160. Quite a performance for shareholders!

But the shareholders were not the only beneficiaries. The company benefited as well by achieving higher operating margins, growing, and providing greater opportunities for employees. Figure 5–8 shows Southwest's operating margins and compares them with the operating margins of the average major airline over a similar period. Figure 5–9 compares the 1995 revenue growth rates for the major airlines.

Value as a management tool can provide the focus management needs to streamline the decision-making process and improve communication of the corporate goals, strategies, and accomplishments. All value flows from the customer who buys the product or service. In the Southwest example, the customers provide the fuel that burns in the value engine. The value they contribute is distributed among the employees, suppliers (aircraft, seats, peanuts, and so on), management, and shareholders.

Value is also the currency of decision making. It allows comparability across businesses, companies, and industries and provides the mechanism to think through and judge the trade-offs management is asked to make.

Southwest chose to fly from Love Field in Dallas as a way to hold down costs and provide convenient access to downtown Dallas. A trade-off Southwest accepted by using Love Field limited their passenger services to the five states that are contiguous to Texas.[1] Another trade-off Southwest accepted involved the inability to provide their passengers with easy connections to other longer-haul carriers because those carriers flew out of Dallas–Fort Worth International Airport, not Love Field.

Today, Southwest's choice may seem obvious because

122

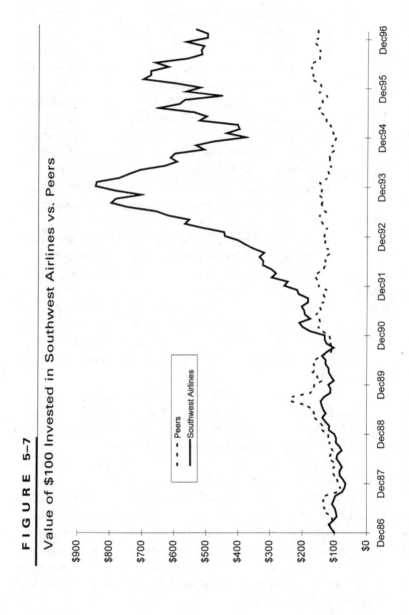

FIGURE 5-7

Value of $100 Invested in Southwest Airlines vs. Peers

FIGURE 5-8

Operating Margin Southwest Airlines and Peers

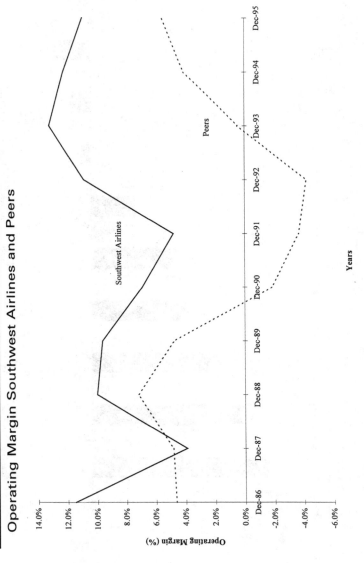

124

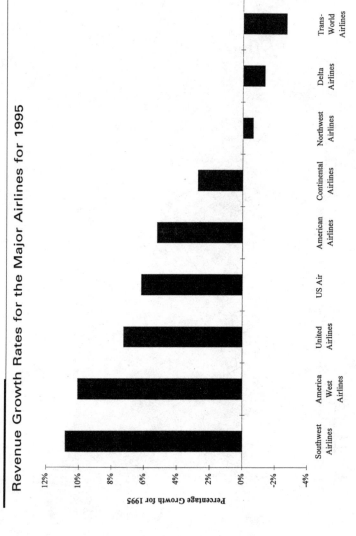

FIGURE 5-9

Revenue Growth Rates for the Major Airlines for 1995

of the success it has enjoyed and the route structure it
has built up. But in the 1970s when that trade-off was
part of the decision to start Southwest and invest money,
it was far from a foregone conclusion that Southwest
would succeed. At that time, Southwest's management
had to weigh the merits of the decision in light of the
value they thought they could create relative to the value
they would lose. Value is an excellent measure for trade-
offs. Value measures capture the capital issues as well
as the income and expense issues and can be compared
relative to investors' expectations for other opportunities
as well as over time.

Southwest now faces similar choices as they expand
their route structure into the northeastern part of the United
States. Their strategy remains unchanged. The management
discipline required, to expand only if expansion is profitable, is the key to Southwest's success for shareholders.

VALUE CREATION IS THE GOAL

When taken together, the results of value management can
help the company build and maintain competitive advantage. Competitive advantage can and does come from many
sources, including people, intellectual capital, technology,
scale, position, and capabilities. Improved decision making
helps a company establish a competitive advantage by making the right decisions and learning from successes and
mistakes more quickly.

Intel is another example of how consistent signals and
alignment improve decision making and drive value creation. Prior to 1984, Intel focused on memory chips and
earned most of its profits the same way as the other semiconductor companies. However, under pressure from the price
collapse of memory chips, Intel identified time to market
and proprietary technology as important sources of competitive advantage.

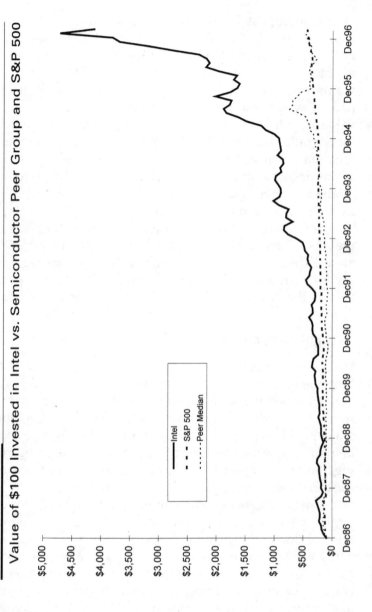

FIGURE 5-10

Value of $100 Invested in Intel vs. Semiconductor Peer Group and S&P 500

Since 1984, Intel has consistently developed the ability to sustain returns by getting microprocessors to market faster than its competitors. This improved decision making resulted in higher returns for both investors and managers. Figure 5–10 shows just how much Intel investors benefited.

MAKE VALUE MANAGEMENT REAL

Business today is more complex than ever, and management is being asked to make trade-offs between conflicting objectives. What better focusing tool for management than a single objective: value? Though appealing as a concept, in reality it is not practical in a large company to have everyone focused on value. Value must be translated into decision-making terms. This is accomplished using the corporate processes to push value management throughout the company in order to improve the focus on strategy execution and to achieve better alignment.

Today, companies are increasing their focus on achieving the corporate objectives. Value management improves communication by defining the objective, clarifying the strategy, and measuring how managers' decisions contribute to executing the strategy and creating value.

CHAPTER 6

Value-Based
Decision Making

The goal of management is to maximize value by executing the company's strategy. Successfully achieving this goal is becoming difficult as business issues become more complex, organizations grow, industries consolidate, and the speed of competition increases. Today, managers are challenged to develop strategies that respond to changing circumstances and to execute those strategies to maintain and build value. Success requires value-based decision making.

To understand how management can meet this very real challenge, we will examine two industries that, on the surface, appear to be at very different starting points in developing and executing strategies to build value. The first industry, banking, is one of the oldest businesses in the world; the second, semiconductors, is one of the newest.

Banks have traditionally relied heavily on people-intensive processes, such as transaction processing, loan approval and review, and retail branches, to conduct business. Semiconductor companies, on the other hand, have relied on a combination of intellectual capital (chip and application design) and capital investment to create value for shareholders.

On the surface, these industries are quite different, with substantially different amounts of capital invested. By 1980, investors had invested $108 billion in the banking industry and $6 billion in the semiconductor industry. However, there are interesting parallels in the challenges these industries face in implementing their strategies.

BANKING

Banking is a good example of an industry undergoing fundamental change and restructuring. In 1981, there were 4,155 banks with federal charters in the United States. In the early 1980s, banking was still shaking off the cobwebs of its highly regulated past and its reliance on local market presence. Banking in the early 1980s was an industry with enormous overcapacity; that is, there were more banks than were necessary to service customers. Many banks entered into the 1980s with too much staff, high-cost positions, and uneconomical processes. However, even with high-cost positions, the banks were still profitable, which bred management complacency.

The number of banks was a function of an earlier day before electronic communications, when regulation supported a local market presence. For example, in Massachusetts, banking laws historically allowed banks to operate in specific counties of the state. Although Cambridge is less than a mile across the Charles River from Boston, banks in Boston were not allowed to have branches in Cambridge because Cambridge is in a different county.[1]

Because banking was historically a local activity, banks were able to charge more for their services and achieve premium pricing for the loans they made. In the 1980s, the old image of the banker and the idea of "banker's hours" from 10 a.m. to 4 p.m. changed substantially as bankers found themselves in a more competitive environment. By 1990, the total number of federally chartered banks had dropped to 3,972, and by 1996 the total number of federally chartered banks stood at 2,732. This represents a consolidation of 29 percent in the industry over 15 years, as shown in Figure 6–1.

Powerful fundamental forces such as economies of scale, access to capital markets, mutual funds, and international funds flow altered the business of banking. Against this backdrop of rapidly evolving change, bankers had to develop strategies and be ready to change their strategy as market conditions shifted. In an environment where change becomes the norm, effective execution of business strategy can make the difference between success and failure.

By 1996, the primary basis for loan pricing (even in the small commercial loan market) had changed from the prime lending rate in the United States to LIBOR.[2] A large percentage of loans for commercial customers were being quoted at a spread over LIBOR, and 60 percent were made below the prime rate. The base rate is no longer a U.S. rate but rather an international standard reflecting the global nature of how funds flow. Figure 6–2 shows the difference between prime and LIBOR rates for the period 1981–1996.

The change in banking profitability during the 1980s was dramatic. Return On Equity (ROE) dropped from 13.7 percent in 1980 to 1.8 percent in 1987 (see Figure 6–3). From 1987 to 1996, the industry responded to the changes, and mergers reduced the number of competitors while the survivors became more efficient.

Wells Fargo became the most profitable money center bank in the 1985–1995 period. It is the preeminent example of a company that responded well to the underlying changes in the banking industry and provides many examples of value-based decision making.

Wells Fargo identified the importance of leveraging its fixed investments in technology. Its efforts placed them in one of the lower cost positions in the industry. Management was not willing to stop at this level of success but instead

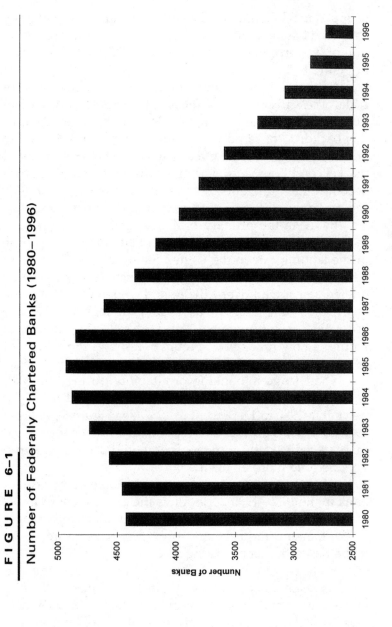

FIGURE 6-1

Number of Federally Chartered Banks (1980–1996)

FIGURE 6-2

Prime Rate and LIBOR (1981–1996)

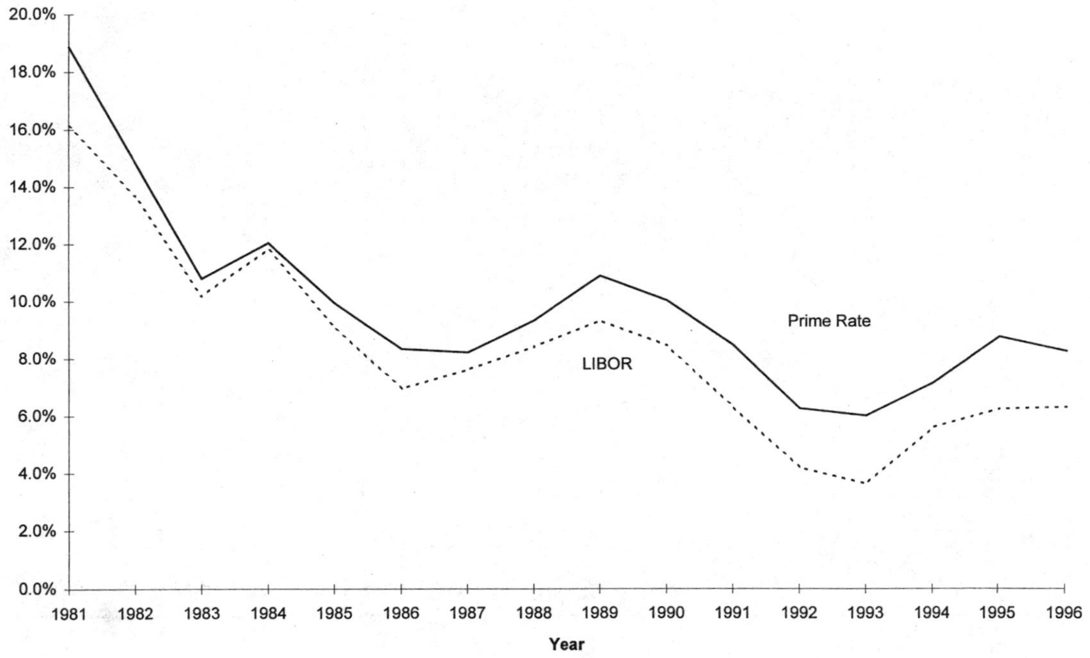

134

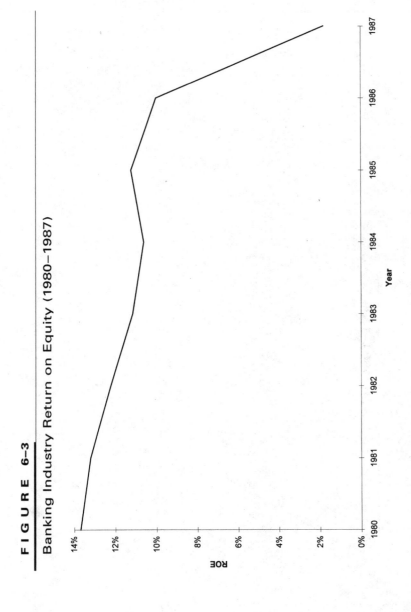

FIGURE 6-3

Banking Industry Return on Equity (1980–1987)

decided to add more value by growing the bank through acquisition. Management reasoned that they could apply their lower cost structure to other banks and create value through a combination of growth, cost reduction, and economies of scale. Wells Fargo was able to use its lower cost position to generate profits, acquire other banks, and mold them into Wells Fargo's cost structure.

The cost-reduction process was not always painless. For example, when Wells Fargo acquired Crocker Bank in 1986 in an acquisition valued at $1.1 billion, Crocker had a much higher cost position than Wells Fargo. After the acquisition of Crocker, Wells Fargo laid off 4,000 people to reduce costs at Crocker. These layoffs were unfortunate, but they dramatize the extent of Wells Fargo's cost advantage when compared to Crocker's. The result was a tremendous increase in the value of Wells Fargo over the period 1986–1996, as shown in Figure 6–4.

SEMICONDUCTORS

In 1981, semiconductor companies were a new industry. This industry had grown from virtually nothing in the 1970s to sales of $13 billion in the 1980s (see Figure 6–5).

The industry was populated by nimble-footed competitors and entrepreneurs, such as Intel, Texas Instruments, Motorola, and Advanced Micro Devices. Change was a constant in the semiconductor industry, and most people inside the industry knew Moore's law, which defined the rate of that change.[3] Figure 6–6 provides evidence of Moore's law.

Semiconductor competitors were ready for change. Although secure in the knowledge that rapid development was normal for semiconductors, industry leaders of that time were not aware of the level of change waiting right around the corner.

Figure 6–7 shows the composition of the semiconductor industry in 1980 by revenue.

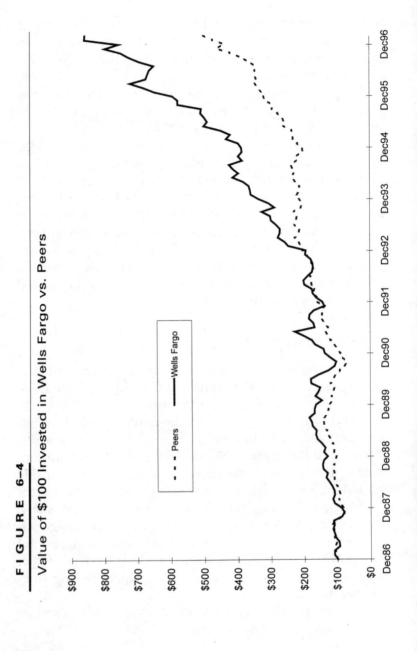

FIGURE 6-4

Value of $100 Invested in Wells Fargo vs. Peers

F I G U R E 6–5

Semiconductor Industry Net Sales

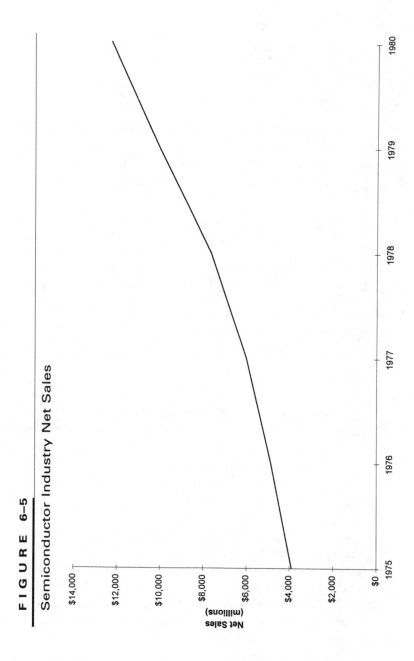

137

FIGURE 6-6

Moore's Law

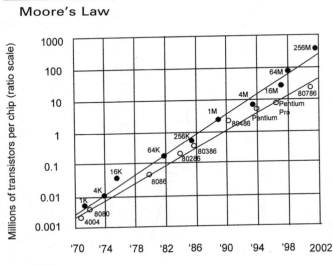

● DRAM memory

○ Intel microprocessor

By 1986, the semiconductor industry was in the tank. Products, such as dynamic random access memory (DRAM), that were profitable in the late 1970s and early 1980s were now not profitable. Investments made by swashbuckling entrepreneurs in plant and equipment to produce the memory chips threatened to bankrupt the industry. What had changed? What had they missed?

The onslaught of Japanese competition and increase in production capacity, in excess of demand, had lead to substantial pricing pressure and lower margins. By 1985, 85 percent of semiconductor manufacturing had moved outside the United States, and companies like Intel had lost their lead. Despite increasing industry sales, profits remained lackluster, as seen in Figure 6–8.

In the semiconductor industry, common wisdom in

Semiconductor Industry Revenue Composition (1980)

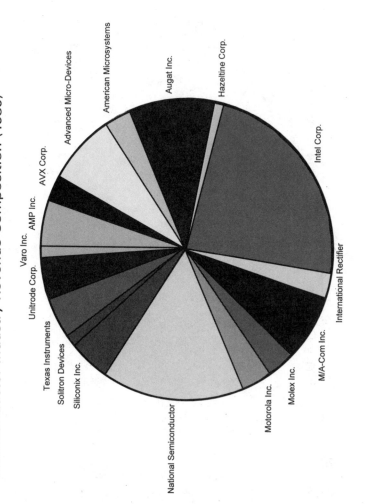

140

FIGURE 6-8

Semiconductor Industry Net Sales and Net Income ($ millions)

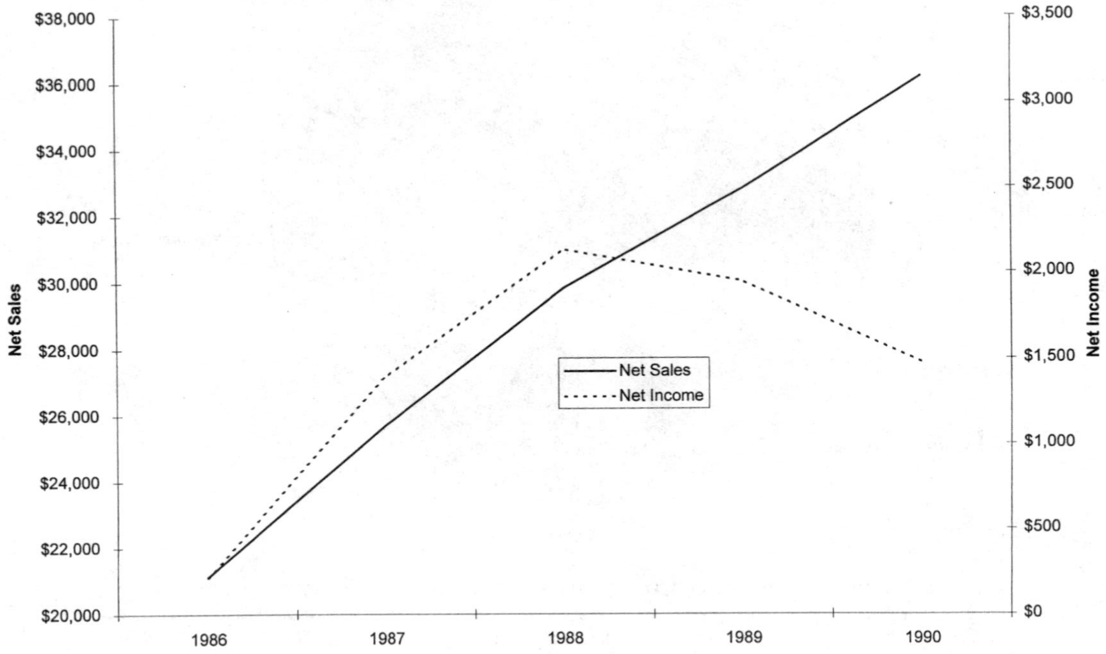

1980 was that the best way to create value was to focus on economies of scale. In memory chips, the ability of a company to earn a return on its investment was a function of how fast the company could achieve economies of scale.[4] A notable example of scale-based competition is Texas Instrument's experience in calculators in the 1970s.

Intel anticipated the downward shift in margins for memory early on and decided to focus on the production of microprocessors. The decision to focus on development of new technology and proprietary microprocessor designs provided a competitive advantage in economies of scale, speed to market, and proprietary technology, allowing them to maintain a greater piece of the value pie.

Semiconductor companies make two types of investments: the capital required to produce the chips, often referred to as fabrication facilities (fabs); and the investment in R&D expense to develop the chip designs. Intel decided to manage for a greater return on their capital investment, and they plotted a strategy to focus on the development of new technology and proprietary microprocessor designs. Intel believed that with this focus they could develop microprocessors and get them to market faster than their competitors. Intel was confident that the combination of speed to market and their proprietary technology would enable them to maintain a greater piece of the value pie.

Moore's law was working dramatically in Intel's favor. If the number of operations conducted in the microprocessor doubled every 18 months, the company that was most effective at the speedy design and time to market of the new microprocessor chips would reap the rewards in the form of higher profitability and generate greater returns for its shareholders. Figure 6–9 illustrates the increase in profitability at Intel as more powerful microprocessors were introduced.

The increased levels of profitability generated higher returns for shareholders and rewarded Intel for its ability

FIGURE 6-9

Net Income and Microprocessor Introduction Dates: Intel

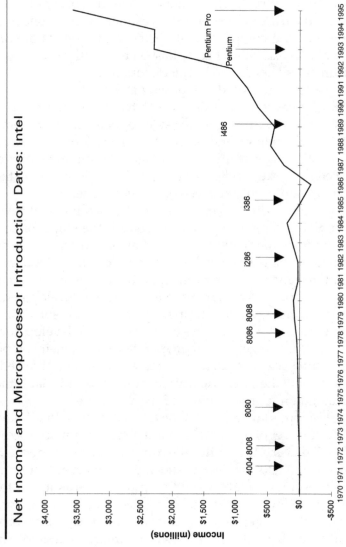

to respond effectively to the changes in the semiconductor industry. Figure 6–10 illustrates Intel's superior returns versus others in its peer group over the period from 1986 through 1996.

These results are not serendipitous; they come from Intel's superior ability to develop strategies and make changes their competitors did not make. Intel was not the only company that foresaw the coming importance of the microprocessor; however, they positioned the company to take advantage of it.

By 1996, Intel had regained its lead, but some of its early competitors had also achieved great success. The industry's success was fueled by the boom in personal computer technologies and the underlying demand for semiconductors in a wide variety of applications, from telephones to home appliances and automobiles.

LESSONS FROM BANKING AND SEMICONDUCTORS

The banking and semiconductor industries represent two ends of the spectrum both in terms of age and their understanding of the speed of change. Banking in 1980 was a mature industry, and the business of banking was conducted in much the same way as it had been 50 years earlier. Corporate bankers maintained their relationships on the golf course, and the volume of loans was the primary measure of a banker's success. In 1980, the transistor was only 32 years old, and semiconductors were a new industry. The speed of change in the semiconductor industry was accelerating as companies found new markets for their products.

Yet both of these industries suffered from many of the same problems. Their strategies were not evolving quickly enough to reflect the fundamental changes going on in their industries. In banking, the combination of financial services

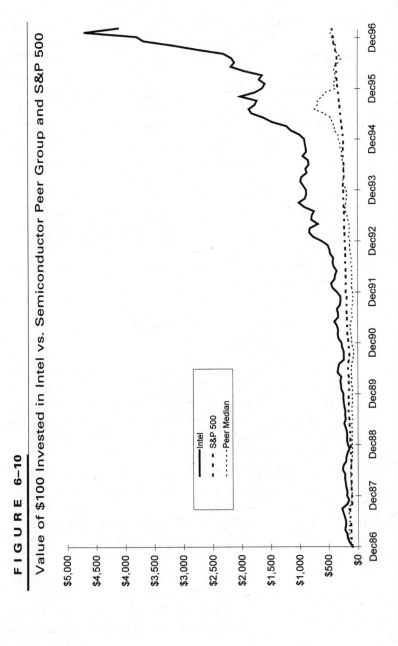

FIGURE 6–10

Value of $100 Invested in Intel vs. Semiconductor Peer Group and S&P 500

144

deregulation, problem loans, and technology were about to alter the industry playing field irrevocably. The semiconductor industry was about to feel the threat of foreign competition. The vast majority of the industry volume, which had been in memory production until this time, was about to move to off-shore producers, while chronic industry overcapacity drove prices and margins lower.

For both industries, strategies during these periods needed to change rapidly to reflect the underlying structural changes taking place. The companies had to respond to marketplace changes and new competitors they encountered. Some companies in the banking industry and others in semiconductors saw the changes coming and responded quickly. These companies sustained less adverse economic consequences than the companies that adapted more slowly [see Figure 6–11(a) and Figure 6–11(b)].

Why were some organizations slower to react than others? Some companies did not see the change coming. Others saw the change but encountered organizational inertia and other roadblocks in attempting to alter the company's direction.

The importance of developing a robust strategy responsive to change cannot be overestimated. However, even with a good strategy, poor execution can torpedo a company's performance. Executing a change in strategy or direction requires a thorough understanding of the new direction, a willingness to change, and the ability to change.

ROADBLOCKS TO CHANGE

Roadblocks are problematic because they keep the strategy from being executed and prevent the company's goals from being attained. Roadblocks create a lack of focus and ambiguity of direction. If managers feel they have encountered a roadblock, they are likely to lose focus on the goal, which

FIGURE 6–11(a)

Value of $100 Invested in Fast/Slow Adapting Companies in the Banking Industry

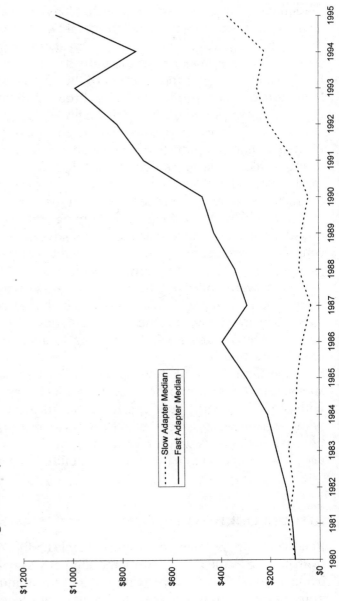

Value of $100 Invested in Fast/Slow Adapting Companies in the
Semiconductor Industry

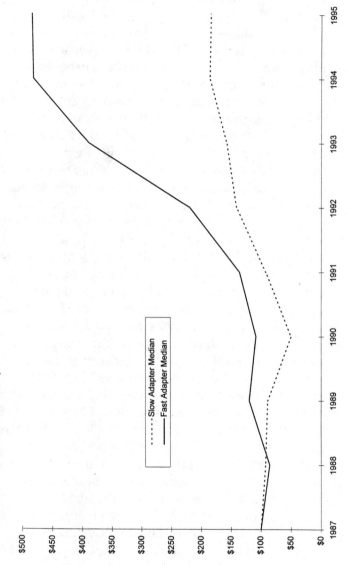

slows progress toward the goal. Instead of focusing on the strategy, they begin focusing on the roadblock.

Many large companies suffer from semipermanent roadblocks. These roadblocks have become self-fulfilling prophesies. Initially, the roadblocks may not have been very significant, but with time they have become a way of life.

Operating managers face semipermanent roadblocks to change in many forms, which can challenge even the most innovative management teams. Consider the operating manager who is asked to balance conflicting priorities by maximizing profit while improving customer service levels. The customer may want faster turnaround time in order to deliver. This can easily lead to increased levels of inventory to have the stock when the customer orders. The increased inventory does not have any direct consequence on "profit," but the higher level of inventory investment reduces the company's return on investment and, when this capital is taken into account, leads to lower levels of profitability.

Staff managers suffer from the same semipermanent roadblocks. The roadblocks may take a slightly different form, but the result is the same. The primary staff functions rely on a clear strategy. Good staff can help execute an unambiguous strategy, but good staff is quickly reduced to ineffectiveness by the lack of clear strategic focus. Lack of clear focus will paralyze most staff organizations. Consider how the lack of focus affects information technology (IT). When the strategy lacks focus, the IT department has difficulty capturing data because the data to be captured is not well defined. This, in turn, leads to poor execution because the information necessary to make the decisions is not available.

The value of breaking down the roadblocks to effective strategy execution is enormous. Success goes to the focused competitor. Given the situation in the industry, you could argue that Intel had no choice but to focus. However, the message is the same: The focused competitor will win the battle. Other semiconductor companies such as Advanced

Micro Devices could have responded and achieved a similar level of focus and performance themselves, but they were slower to move out of the starting blocks.

The contrast is dramatic and is replayed in industry after industry. On the one hand, we find the focused, nimble-footed competitor capable of responding to the challenges and creating value for shareholders. On the other hand, we find the majority of the industry complacent in the status quo.

WHAT CREATES ROADBLOCKS?

The greatest roadblock to successful strategy execution is lack of focus. Lack of focus can occur for three reasons:

1. Lack of a coherent strategy to provide direction to the company.
2. The push and pull of conflicting priorities. Each priority may be well-intentioned, but together they are pointing the company in different directions simultaneously.
3. Incrementalism.

In 1990, IBM was a company lacking a coherent strategy. IBM had become the most profitable company in the world because of mainframe computers and had developed a very effective organization to develop, manufacture, and market mainframe computers, which are known in the industry as "big iron." IBM wrote the book on how to market technology through a direct sales force. Many of the senior executives at the minicomputer companies, such as Digital, Data General, Prime, and others, cut their teeth in IBM's salesforce training program.

By 1990, the environment had changed. Marketing technology through a direct sales force was not as profitable because of increased competition and pressure on margins. Change was accelerating with the advent of personal computers and workstations. IBM was very successful in introducing their first PC in 1983 but was having difficulty converting their early personal computer success to a sustainable advantage. By 1990, IBM had lost enough opportunities to be well behind in market share for personal computers. In minicomputers, IBM had bet heavily on the AS400 and had achieved only moderate success.

The cost to sell, support, and service the smaller computers was not supported by gross profit. This lead to an interesting problem, and IBM found itself confused for the first time about how to maintain profitability in the face of these dramatic industry changes. Although the number of employees declined from 405,000 at its peak, the company was still handicapped with a huge workforce numbering 373,000 in 1990. The number of employees was not only a cost to be reckoned with but also a challenge because if management was going to succeed in changing strategy, they had to shift the direction of all employees. The very strengths in direct sales that had made the company successful had become roadblocks to future success. In 1990, IBM was stumbling forward, an industrial behemoth weighted down by the vestiges of its own success, handicapped by its own capabilities, and unable to respond to the need for a coherent strategy to address changes in the industry.

AT&T is another company that lacked focus in the early 1990s. AT&T went through a series of acquisitions, buying NCR for $7.5 billion in 1991 and buying McCaw Cellular for $11.5 billion in 1994. AT&T was challenged to assimilate these acquisitions and simultaneously respond to the increasing competitive threat in the core long-distance business. MCI, Sprint, and a host of other less-known long distance providers were chipping away at AT&T's market share for long distance. Figure 6–12 shows AT&T's loss of share over the period 1984–1993.

At the same time AT&T was making acquisitions, the cost to maintain its position in long distance was increasing.

FIGURE 6–12

AT&T Long Distance Market Share

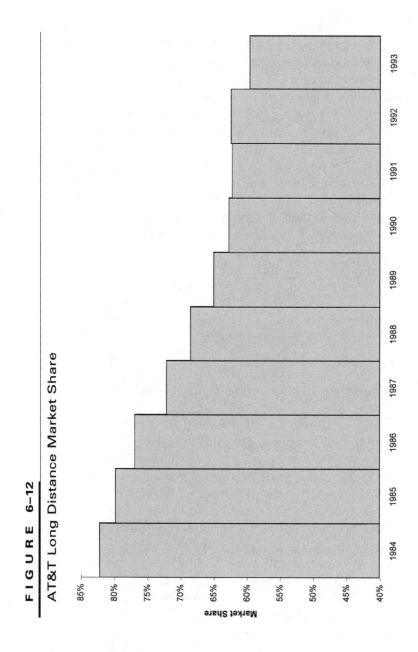

AT&T increased the amount of marketing expenditures to
$23 billion in 1995. Challenges to a core source of profitabil-
ity would keep most companies focused, but AT&T demonstrated its inability to focus by conducting numerous major
acquisitions during this same period. NCR was the largest
single disaster and accounted for enormous losses during
the time it was owned by AT&T. AT&T concluded that
NCR was beyond repair and decided to spin it off. This
trail of acquisitions and lack of focus was very costly for
shareholders, with AT&T providing meager returns for
shareholders during the period 1986–1996. Figure 6–13 illustrates AT&T's value created during this period compared
with others in the industry. In 1995 AT&T announced it
would split into three companies and, shareholders ap-
plauded the anticipated increase in focus.

The message from IBM and AT&T is clear: Success
requires well-conceived and well-executed strategies. While
IBM and AT&T present infamous examples of miscued and
poorly executed strategies, the same issues apply in every
company. Lack of focus due to conflicting priorities can be
devastating to any company, for example, if management
places emphasis on improving profitability and earning
higher returns while at the same time pushing a business
strategy that requires growth in capital investment. In this
example, the two priorities are in conflict because the desire
for higher returns will encourage managers to reduce capital
investment while the priority for growth in capital expenditures will encourage capital spending. Conflicts such as
these become especially troublesome when the company's
corporate processes (planning, budgeting, compensation,
and resource allocation) send conflicting signals to employees about the company's priorities (see Figure 6–14).

Companies that find themselves lacking focus and direction usually perform poorly. Prominent examples include conglomerates Tenneco, Textron, and Litton, where
value creation for shareholders has lagged behind the norm.

FIGURE 6–13

Value of $100 Invested in AT&T and Peers

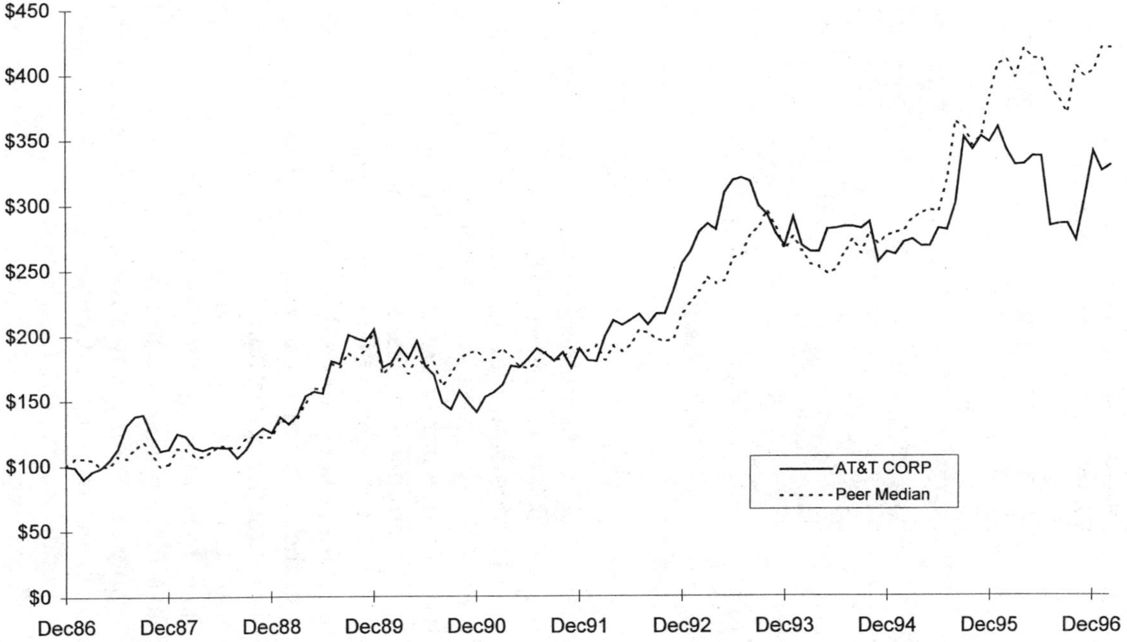

Legend:
— AT&T CORP
······· Peer Median

Y-axis: $0, $50, $100, $150, $200, $250, $300, $350, $400, $450

X-axis: Dec86, Dec87, Dec88, Dec89, Dec90, Dec91, Dec92, Dec93, Dec94, Dec95, Dec96

F I G U R E   6–14

Examples of Conflicting Signals

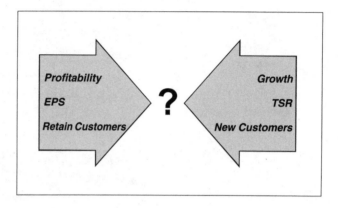

Figure 6–15 compares value creation for conglomerates and the S&P 500 over the period 1979–1989.

The company that is protected by a corporate umbrella is more likely to be slow to respond. In any profitable industry, a competitor or potential competitor is always willing to take profitable business away and is often looking to do just that. Companies that do not respond quickly to threats to their market shares will lose out. The corporate umbrella over the operating business often acts as a security blanket, providing the perception that the business is protected and insulated from competitive threats. Conglomerates are less likely to be focused if for no other reason than they simply have more businesses to track and understand. The more nimble the company, relative to its competitors, the greater the chance for success. Conversely, the slower the company responds, the greater the chance of failure.

One conglomerate that has succeeded in managing for value is Thermo Electron. Thermo Electron enforces the value mind-set and discipline into all the companies in its portfolio by using a combination of value-oriented pro-

Value of $100 Invested in Conglomerate Median vs. S&P 500

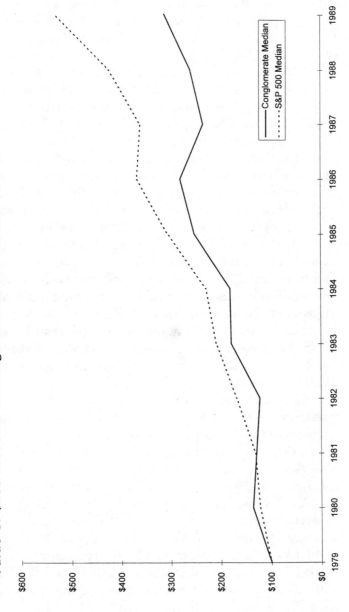

cesses, value-based decision making, and a market discipline supported with a strategy of partial spin-offs to shareholders. Figure 6–16 illustrates Thermo Electron's return over the last five years.

Similarly, the company that changes incrementally is unlikely to be a fast competitor. This does not imply that a company must be foolhardy to be successful because there is plenty of time for a considered response. The company that lacks focus is unlikely to respond either quickly or consistently and will find itself at a disadvantage. Management can be lulled into a sense of complacency by the notion that incremental change will fix the problem and that the organization will self-correct if given enough time to readjust to the new operating environment. But nothing could be further from the truth. It is impossible to leap the Grand Canyon in a series of small jumps. Incrementalism is one of the greatest risks of all because it costs the most precious resource: time. Wasted time may not make a difference in an industry where competition and change are not important. However, in industries where change is the norm, incrementalism increases the time required to change and reduces the company's adaptation to change because the lure of inertia is often too great.

General Motors is an example of a company that suffered from incrementalist management. Incrementalism was a great enemy at this company because it lead to the belief that no radical change was necessary. Business as usual sufficed as long as management responded incrementally to any need for change in the organization. This belief cost General Motors' CEO Robert Stempel his job. General Motors' strategy of incremental change was not adequate to set the company on the road to responding to the changes in the auto industry. In the 1980s, General Motors had lost 10 percentage points in market share in the United States and was faced in 1990 with a disadvantageous cost position and nagging quality problems. Figure 6–17 illustrates the market share loss.

F I G U R E 6–16

Value of $100 Invested in Thermo Electron

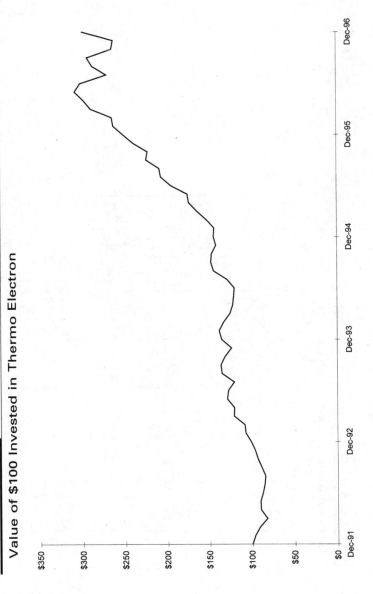

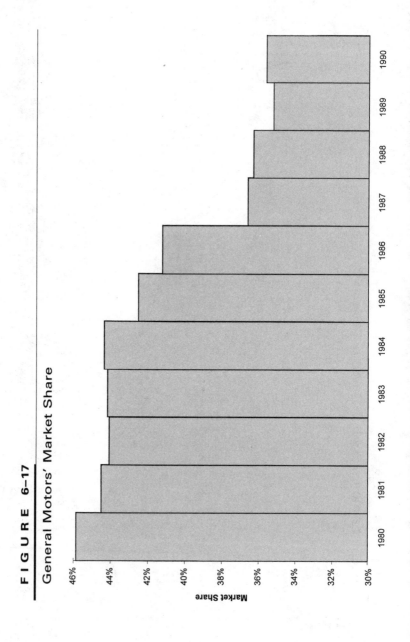

General Motors' Market Share

One response by GM management to the market share loss was a diversification strategy. But the diversification strategy attempted by former GM CEO Roger Smith through the acquisition of Hughes and EDS did not cure the basic problem. The need for change was not incremental but extraordinary. Incremental change assumes the company has the time to make the change. In many cases, this strategy is just what the doctor ordered. But in the case where the speed of change in an industry is accelerating and rules of competitive engagement are changing, incremental change is often insufficient.

Specialty publishing in the late 1980s also faced a technological and competitive challenge. The technological challenge changed the way information was to be gathered, analyzed, categorized, published, and delivered to subscribers. Ironically, the competitive challenge was a result of the change in technology, which drove down the cost of entering the business. New entrants were able to distribute the same information in alternative media at a much lower cost than the traditional face-to-face hard-copy distribution. These fundamental shifts in the competitive dynamic called for an aggressive response.

Commerce Clearing House (CCH) was a leader in the specialty publishing business in the late 1980s. It had built a very successful franchise in their market and was known as the leader in their business. But by the early 1990s, CCH was facing serious threats to their business franchise from industry consolidation. Competition was increasing quickly, customers were rapidly changing to alternative suppliers, and technology was a potential threat.

Commerce Clearing House was founded in 1892 and by 1991 had grown into a $700 million sales company with six businesses: legal publishing, international legal publishing, computer tax processing, legal services, library reference materials, and stock quotations in the form of the "pink sheets." CCH's business grew rapidly during the 1970s and

1980s because of increased demand from lawyers and accountants driven by the increased complexity of the U.S. tax code. Because the market perceived their offerings as high value added, price was not a significant factor in the sale of the product. The company's success peaked in 1988 when the company was valued in the market at $1.25 billion. But the next few years were not pleasant for the company.

Three fundamental changes shook CCH's business, reducing the sales, the profitability, and the value of the company:

1. Competition heated up for CCH. Foreign competitors, most notably Thomson Corp., acquired many of CCH's competitors and began a serious push for market share, using lower prices as a weapon.

2. Customers became more price sensitive as the economy entered the downturn of 1989 and more alternatives became available.

3. Technology began to change and threatened to replace both the way CCH gathered and processed data and the way they delivered products to their customers. Personal computers threatened to replace CCH's service bureau tax-return business (which was based on mainframe technology), and competing technologies such as CD-ROMs threatened the company's high-fixed-cost print publishing business.

The company faced internal challenges as well. Because the company had no planning or budgeting systems, measuring performance was difficult at best. By 1991, CCH was beginning to lose share and volume in its core businesses. The success of the company had led to a sleepy management culture that was not ready for the changes they confronted.

In 1991, with revenues flat or falling in the core businesses and profitability dropping dramatically, investors responded by reducing the market value of the company's stock from $35 to $18 per share. The CCH board decided things had to change if CCH was going to survive and respond to the changes in the marketplace.

In 1991, the board chose Oakleigh Thorne as the new CEO to lead the change process based on his proven success in turning around the profitability of the Legal Information Services division. The board gave him the mandate to overhaul the company and improve operations. Over the next two years, Oakleigh lead an aggressive change program that redesigned the company and resulted in CCH's successful turnaround. In the process, he invested $300 million in the company. He redefined the business, changing it from publishing to providing information tools for the company's customers, which reduced their costs. He sold the noncore businesses and closed all but one of the company's printing plants, reducing the number of employees from 7,500 to 4,900.

To accomplish his goal of turning the company around, Thorne installed performance measures in managerial reporting and financial reporting systems and linked them to the compensation system. He included not only financial measures in the compensation but also measures of customer satisfaction and other non-single-period measures. He changed the compensation program from a tenure-based plan design to a performance-based plan and instituted an option program for the top 40 managers in the company (almost all new). The stock option program was designed to turbocharge the turnaround by providing the 14 top executives with a significant incentive (20 times annual salary) and the next 26 senior managers with an incentive of 14 times annual salary to improve the company's value.

The turnaround happened even faster than hoped, and by 1994 the company was beating profit expectations. In 1995, with income running over 20 percent ahead of expectations, the company's market value grew quickly. In the fall of 1995, CCH was approached by two potential suitors, one of which (Wolter Kluwer NV) ended up buying the company for $1.9 billion, or $55.55 per share, at the end of November.

CCH saw the threat of a rapidly changing competitive environment, realized the company's survival depended on changing the way they did business, and responded. The results speak for themselves. Oakleigh Thorne (former CEO of CCH) emphasizes the importance of being able to execute the company's strategy as follows:

> If I had to attribute the success of our turnaround to the execution of the strategy or the strategy itself, I would say execution accounted for 80 percent of our success. We had businesses where our strategies were excellent but we failed to execute properly and the strategy created no value, and other businesses where the strategy was okay but not great and execution was excellent, and those businesses created a lot of value. The greatest strategy in the world does not help you if the customer is calling with the 13th billing complaint this year.

Incrementalism is appropriate in industries where the pace of change is slow and the competitive landscape is stable. In industries where the pace of change is rapid and/or the competitive landscape is rapidly changing, incrementalism involves greater risks than benefits. One way to think about the speed of change is to compare it to the life cycle of investment in the industry. If the rate of change is greater than the industry life cycle, incremental change is probably not worth the risk, and bolder, more timely action is required (see Figure 6–18).

HOW TO OVERCOME ROADBLOCKS

Assume a company knows it needs to change direction to respond to competition and has a strategy that addresses the necessary change. If the company's management focuses

FIGURE 6-18

Matrix of Industry Life Cycle and Rate of Change

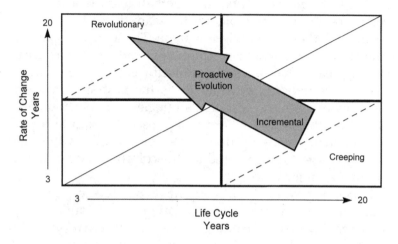

on the right strategy, execution will follow, but if there is confusion over focus, a focus on conflicting objectives, or the wrong focus, the company will face a serious hurdle responding to the new competitive environment.

Successful strategy execution is all about identifying and overcoming roadblocks. Strategy execution requires that individuals understand the strategy and how they can affect it. Companies that understand what is required and how they are going to achieve their strategic goals have an advantage over their competitors. They have the capability to execute their strategy in a timely fashion. Some companies do it well, while other companies in the same industry lack the ability to get their strategies implemented.

Strategy can only be executed if people understand what they are being asked to do and how they are going to do it. The strategy must be translated into the operating decisions that managers are making daily.

A good strategy is essential for value creation. However, a good strategy by itself is not sufficient to create value. The strategy must be successfully executed for its value to be realized. Like the football team whose coach prepares a great game plan, if the team doesn't follow the plan well, they won't win the game. The ability to execute the strategy is a source of competitive advantage as great if not greater than the strategy itself (see Figure 6–19).

Understanding what to do is the first step in good strategy execution. Too often, strategies are poorly understood by the people who are supposed to execute them. The company ends up doing business as usual while the strategy is best remembered for the colorful binders sitting on management's bookshelves.

Some people think slapping a pay-for-performance plan into the company's incentive program is the antidote for bad strategy execution and poor performance. The attitude seems to be "If I can just get some of that economic value added [or a similar measure], then we'll get the behavior we want." If you emphasize pay for performance, it is true you will see some benefit in the form of behavioral change, but

FIGURE 6–19

Strategy and Execution

	Strategy	
	Good	Bad
Execution — Good	Intel Cisco Coca-Cola Microsoft	General Motors Phillips Electronics
Execution — Bad	America On-Line WMX Technologies	M-Tech AT&T Apple Quaker Oats

the benefit will be limited and may be short-lived. Changing behavior is more complicated than installing a new pay-for-performance plan; it requires a thorough understanding of the company's strategy. Often, compensation and pay-for-performance are the first steps in changing behavior.

Once a company's strategy is thoroughly understood, successful execution depends on identifying and overcoming roadblocks. The complete job of overcoming the roadblocks to strategy execution is a four-step process, illustrated in Figure 6–20.

Step 1: Identify Performance Measures, Develop Compensation Systems, and Define Pay for Performance

Chapter 7 will discuss a process for selecting an appropriate performance measure(s). The important issue in selecting a performance measure(s) is to choose the one that will work inside your company and send the right management decision-making signals. Following the performance-measure selection process in Chapter 7 will help guarantee the measure you use is suited for the purpose.

In Chapter 8, we will discuss how to develop a compensation system that addresses the company's strategy and rewards the desired behavior while aligning with the strategy. Intelligent selection of a compensation design is a powerful tool for strategy execution.

Pay for performance is the link between the performance measure(s) selected and the compensation plan chosen. Establishing the relationship between performance and pay is an important opportunity to set the correct relationship between risk and reward in the plan and send the right messages to managers in the organization.

Of course it is possible to choose an "off the shelf" measure such as economic value added and install it in the performance-measurement and compensation plans of the

Overcoming Roadblocks to Strategy Execution

Communication

Manage the Value Drivers

Identify Value Drivers

Performance Measures, Compensation, and Pay for Performance

company. Some prominent advocates of single measures even promise management increases in their stock price for simply announcing the choice of the measure. This is rubbish. There is no evidence to support the claim that a single performance measure will lead to higher stock price. *Fortune* magazine has glamorized the use of economic value added at Coca-Cola and tried to attribute the bulk of Coke's success to the measure. Coke's success is a combination of many years of good decision making. While economic value added supports Coke's decision making, it creates no value in and of itself because it is merely a measure of the company's results. Much more important is a thoughtfully selected measure and the signals that measure and compensation program send to management. These signals will remain day in and day out and influence behavior in the company and the quality of the decisions made.

Companies that take this first step in the process are likely to achieve a portion of their value potential. Linking the performance and compensation into a pay-for-performance orientation will help focus management. However, to maximize value, you must include the strategy; it is the strategy that gets you the majority of the value opportunity. The really successful value creators—Intel, CCH, Wells Fargo—have gone beyond merely establishing a new set of performance measures and have focused on improving decision making.

Step 2: Identify the Value Drivers

Value drivers are the operating factors with the greatest influence on operating and financial results. Our definition goes well beyond the results and incorporates the entire decision-making dynamic.

Strategy is too abstract for most people in the company. Value drivers help make the strategy real at a level of specificity that is both meaningful and actionable. The definition of value drivers must include important aspects of the operating decisions. Value drivers are also used to understand nonfinancial operating measures. These operating value drivers define the strategy to people in the organization and ultimately lead to behavior changes.

Value drivers occur in all parts of the company, including product development, manufacturing, marketing, sales, and staff functions. The prevalence of value drivers in each function will vary by industry. For example, the software industry has relatively fewer value drivers in manufacturing and more in product development than capital intensive industries like automotive or steel. Figures 6–21(a) and 6–21(b) provide examples of value drivers.

Step 3: Manage the Value Drivers

Identifying the value drivers of the business is helpful, but value maximization comes from using them in the decision-making and corporate processes. Companies are often caught up in quarterly financial reporting cycles and make decisions based on financial information. Making important decisions using financial reporting information is like driving a car while looking through a rear view mirror. Financial reporting tells us where we've been, not where we're going. What we should care about is where we're going and making decisions that support our direction. Once we have identified the value drivers, we can use them to build a forward-looking managerial reporting system that helps us seek out the front windshield and understand how the decisions we make are likely to affect our progress.

Value drivers provide an opportunity to build a strategic/operating managerial reporting system that can be used for decision making, improving the strategy development and execution process.

Financial and managerial reporting is likely to suffer from serious incremental problems because measures of

F I G U R E 6-21(a)

Examples of Operational Value Drivers—The Income Statement

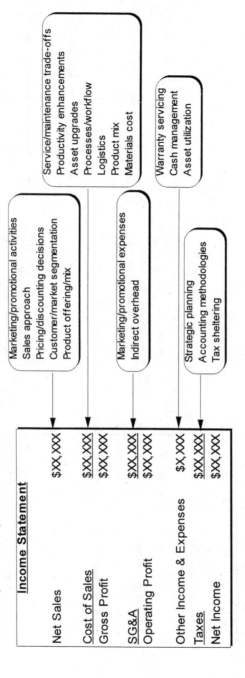

Income Statement

Net Sales	$XX,XXX
Cost of Sales	$XX,XXX
Gross Profit	$XX,XXX
SG&A	$XX,XXX
Operating Profit	$XX,XXX
Other Income & Expenses	$X,XXX
Taxes	$XX,XXX
Net Income	$XX,XXX

Net Sales:
- Marketing/promotional activities
- Sales approach
- Pricing/discounting decisions
- Customer/market segmentation
- Product offering/mix

Cost of Sales:
- Service/maintenance trade-offs
- Productivity enhancements
- Asset upgrades
- Processes/workflow
- Logistics
- Product mix
- Materials cost

SG&A:
- Marketing/promotional expenses
- Indirect overhead

Other Income & Expenses:
- Warranty servicing
- Cash management
- Asset utilization

Taxes:
- Strategic planning
- Accounting methodologies
- Tax sheltering

FIGURE 6-21(b)

Examples of Operational Value Drivers—The Balance Sheet

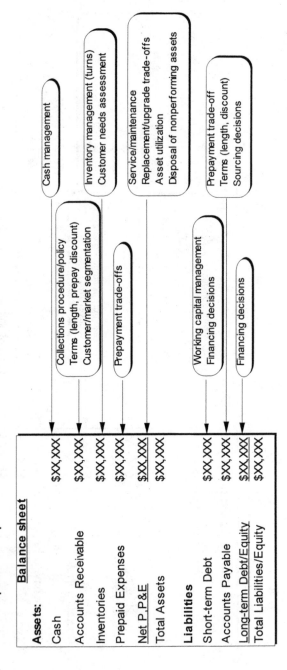

performance are added over time. Management reporting becomes a confusing patchwork of potentially conflicting measures that can be and are used to justify any decision management elects to make.

Step 4: Improve Communication

The effectiveness of the strategy is limited by the participants' understanding of the value drivers, the performance measures, compensation, how they are related to one another, and the signals they send for management decision making. This understanding is a crucial building block to strategy execution. The strategy and the execution of the strategy are only as good as management's ability to communicate its strategy in meaningful terms to the team being asked to execute it. Team-based metaphors are useful here because most businesses run on a team concept: If the team does not know what play (strategy) is being run or how they fit into the play while being expected to contribute to the success of the play (strategy execution), the chances for excellent strategy execution are vastly diminished.

WHY MAKE THE EXTRA EFFORT?

Value-based decision making is not a quick fix. If you want to maximize value, you have to go beyond the simple, pat, off-the-shelf solutions. Installing a pay-for-performance program gets you 20 percent of the way to value-based decision making. If you are interested in getting the other 80 percent, you must improve your understanding of the company's strategy and make that strategy meaningful to the decision makers. This means translating the company's strategy into the value drivers of the business. The companies that have achieved this level of understanding and capability have worked hard to make their strategies successful and have been rewarded accordingly (see Figure 6–22).

FIGURE 6-22

Value of $100 Invested in Industry Leaders vs. Industry Median Value Creation

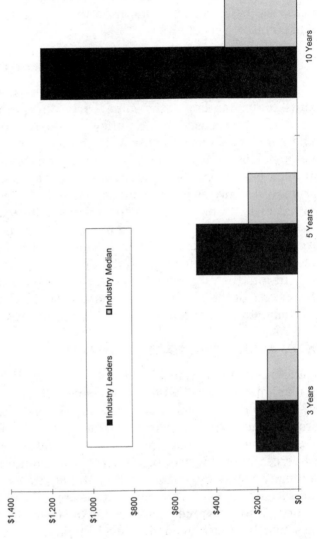

Performance
Measures

Performance measures are one of the most misused management tools in business. Poorly chosen performance measures routinely create the wrong signals for managers, leading to poor decisions and subpar results. There are huge hidden costs to misused performance measures. Shareholders foot the bill each day in the form of wasted resources, overinvestment, acquisitions that don't pay off, and so on. It is not that management is poor. It is simply that performance measures are pushing them to do the wrong things.

Traditional performance-measurement systems were originally constructed at a time when decision making was focused at the center of the organization and responsibilities for decision making were very clearly defined. These performance-measurement systems were designed to measure accountability to ensure that people "met their budget" and followed orders. Most performance-measurement systems have little to do with the company's strategy and often incent management to either make the wrong decision or, after making the right decision, to plead for exceptions to the measurement system. Why are performance measures

so misused? Part of the answer lies in three myths surrounding performance measurement:

1. Growing quarterly earnings per share is all that matters.
2. Accounting measures tell the whole story.
3. You can manage anything solely with financial reporting methods.

These three myths are all based on the common belief that accounting is the only measure of performance.

MYTH 1: GROWING QUARTERLY EARNINGS PER SHARE IS ALL THAT MATTERS

Company after company sacrifices itself on the altar of quarterly earnings per share (EPS) growth because they believe
that investors place a higher value on companies that consistently increase their earnings per share.

This mistaken belief leads to the application of some
rather fascinating and creative accounting practices when
it comes time to deliver quarterly earnings-per-share results
to Wall Street. Managing quarterly earnings encompasses
the entire range of accounting practices, including but not
limited to the timing of revenue recognition, inventory re-
evaluations, deferred charges, and other accounting approaches.

These accounting practices range from benign to overly
aggressive. Examples include CEOs who insist on excessive
write-downs that are later reversed. This tactic is particularly prevalent in the quarter just after a new CEO is ap-
pointed. Pension accounting offers another area for fine-
tuning earnings, as does tax accounting across periods and
jurisdictions. Transfer pricing is one way to maximize tax
advantages between countries or jurisdictions. The tempta-
tion to speed up or delay revenue recognition leads some
companies to delay or advance invoicing at the end of the

quarter. Costs can be managed by changing inventory procedures, changing production schedules, shipping different product mixes, and changing billing practices. Depreciation can be controlled through the timing of capital expenditures, and expenses can always be delayed or moved forward. These are just a few of the earnings-management strategies being used today. Managing quarterly earnings is fast becoming one of the main jobs of the senior management in many public companies. The exact tactics vary from one industry to the next, but the purpose remains the same: to manage the quarterly earnings so management can meet its budgetary targets. There are three reasons not to overmanage quarterly earnings:

1. Overmanaging earnings can come back to haunt you.
2. Investors are not idiots; the sophisticated ones see through the game.
3. Focus on managing for value.

The first reason for not overmanaging quarterly earnings follows Newton's second law of physics. In the same way that Newton's law of gravity recognizes that anything that goes up must come down, earnings that are artificially managed today will be forced down in the future.

The second reason not to overmanage earnings is that investors often recognize when earnings are artificially inflated or deflated. Sophisticated investors want to know whether the results are sustainable. Large institutional investors will tell you they look at the quality of the earnings, not just the earnings themselves. An example of investors' abilities to look beyond the numbers to the quality of the earnings is seen in the movement of IBM's stock price. In the earnings release in October of 1996, IBM's earnings were up, and earnings per share growth came in above Wall Street's expectations. The consensus earnings estimate among the security analysts was $2.40 per share; IBM reported earnings for the quarter of $2.45 per share, which was 5 cents above the consensus estimate. Yet the stock opened down three points after the earnings were announced. Why? The mix of the earnings was not anticipated, and the underlying profit margins on IBM's mainframe business continued to show erosion. Although the company was able to cover the earnings shortfall from other sources, the announcement demonstrates how effective investors are at looking beyond the quarterly earnings numbers to the underlying fundamentals.

Earnings are not the only indicators of value. Earnings represent the company's ability to generate profit from sales given the capital the company is employing. Quarterly earnings only represent a small portion of a company's value. For the S&P 500, earnings in the next five years represented only 21 percent of value.[1] If earnings over the short/medium term are only 21 percent of a company's value, why are investors so focused on quarterly earnings? The answer lies in the signal that quarterly earnings send about the profitability of the company. Investors don't have crystal balls, and information about future expectations is hard to obtain.

Benjamin Graham put earnings in perspective when he wrote: "First, in our opinion, current earnings play neither a definitive nor a constant role in stock price."[2]

The third reason not to overmanage earnings is less obvious but far more profound. Earnings management will get you precisely nowhere in terms of creating value in the long run and may actually destroy value. Investors price the company's stock to deliver the earnings growth rate the company is managing. If the company is managing to a rate of growth less than the company could achieve, management is systematically advising investors to undervalue the company. On the other hand, if management is focused on an earnings growth rate that is not sustainable and the evidence becomes clear to investors, they will reprice the

company's stock downward to reflect those lower expectations. There is little reason to overmanage earnings if the
purpose of the company is to create value through good
decision making in the long run.

Richard Sloan, a professor at the Wharton School of
Management, examined 30 years of stock market data and
found that, although it takes three years for the market to
catch on, the price of a stock with manipulated earnings
will fall to the level predicted by the company's cash flow.[3]

Like most myths, this one is built on a basic truth.
Investors place importance on earnings growth. However,
they are looking for more than just earnings growth. For
evidence, refer to Figure 7–1, which illustrates the growth
in earnings per share (EPS) relative to price-to-earnings
(P/E) multiples for the S&P 400 Industrials. The data contains a lot of noise, but you can see there is a general trend:
The higher the earnings growth rate, the higher the valuation.

There is more to the valuation of companies than earnings growth. Take the year 1995, for example. When you
look at the earnings growth rates for each of the companies
in the S&P 400 Industrials and compare them with the
P/E multiples the market used to value the companies, you
find very little correlation between the earnings growth and
the P/E multiples. The obvious conclusion is that there must
be more to the story than earnings growth.

There is little support in the data to suggest that higher
earnings per share growth correlates with higher values,
yet the amount of the difference in valuations for similar
companies with similar earnings growth rates is striking.
For example, two companies with similar earnings growth
rates are Microsoft and Intel. Each company is growing
rapidly, but they are valued very differently (see Figure
7-2). Why? Each company is very successful, but the amount
of capital required for growth is quite different. Intel has
huge fixed-capital investments in future technology, and

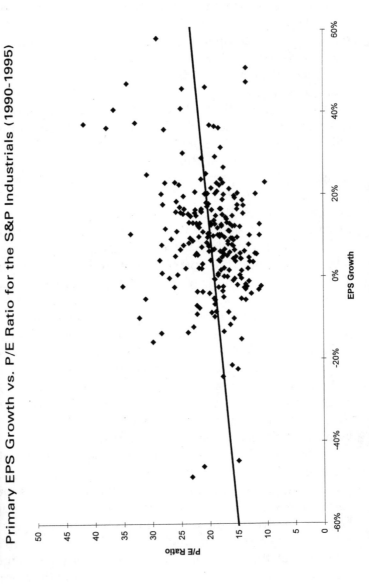

FIGURE 7-1

Primary EPS Growth vs. P/E Ratio for the S&P Industrials (1990-1995)

FIGURE 7-2

Primary EPS Growth vs. P/E Ratio for the S&P Industrials (1990–1995)

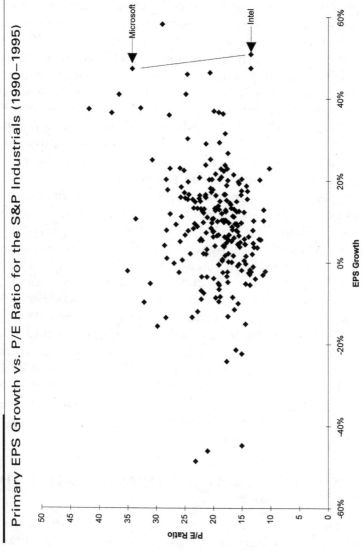

they must earn a return on these investments. Investors are positive about Intel but remain skeptical about the company's ability to continue earning the same return on new investments that it has earned on past investments. If investors believed that Intel's current growth rate will continue and the company will earn the same returns in the future, they would value Intel stock at $370 per share. Instead, the company was valued at $131 per share at the end of 1996.

Using a discounted cash flow valuation, we can explain Intel's stock price based on performance and compare it to the high, low, and closing stock price for each year. This comparison is illustrated in Figure 7–3.

Another common management pitfall concerns over-dilutive acquisitions. Any acquisition purchased at a price greater than the adjusted book value of the acquired company will dilute earnings due to the amortization of intangibles. Is an acquisition that dilutes earnings the right acquisition? The answer to this question lies not in a consideration of earnings dilution but in a consideration of whether or not acquiring the target company is the right business decision.

Management focuses on earnings growth under the mistaken belief that growing EPS is more important than anything else, but that is not true. EPS is only one indicator of financial performance, and the growth in EPS is shorthand for the financial performance of the company. There is much more to performance than EPS and much more to financial performance than EPS.

MYTH 2 : ACCOUNTING MEASURES TELL THE WHOLE STORY

The second myth, like the first, has some truth to it. Accounting does tell a story but not the complete story. Accounting systems tell us about past performance because accounting is a retrospective measure of financial results. Double-entry bookkeeping was first devised by the Franciscan Friar Luca

Intel Actual vs. Predicted Stock Price DCFS Model

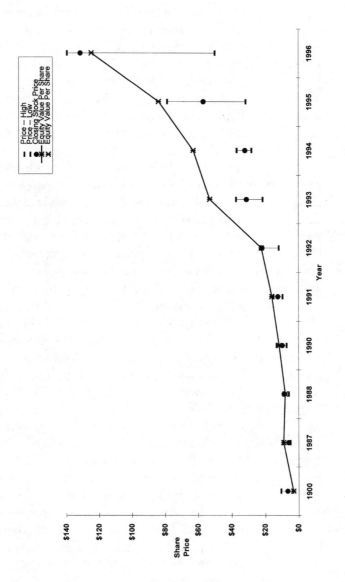

Pacioli in 1494.[4] Since that time, accounting-based measures of performance have taken root as the predominant mechanism to measure performance in business. Accounting measures of performance became widely accepted after World War II and were viewed as a way to manage complex multiple product businesses, which were fast becoming the norm in the 1950s. Until then, the typical measures of performance had been measures such as output, volume, products sold, sales growth, and income growth.

ITT was one of the early advocates of accounting-based performance measures during Harold Geneen's tenure as CEO. ITT began as International Telephone and Telegraph Company, a telephone company focused on developing telephone service in Latin America. At the end of WWII, ITT began an aggressive expansion program that lead to acquisitions of such unrelated businesses as Sheraton Hotels and Hartford Insurance. ITT expanded from a single Latin American telephone business in 1946 to 350 businesses in 1977. By 1977, ITT employed 375,000 people in 80 countries. Geneen believed that financial performance measures gave him enough information about the performance of a business to effectively run a conglomerate containing 250 profit centers. He held monthly performance review meetings during which he thoroughly analyzed the performance of each business unit. These marathon monthly review sessions averaged 12 hours. Each session reviewed all the ITT business units for their performance. In addition, each month one unit was chosen for an in-depth performance review. During these in-depth reviews, the business' ratios were scrutinized. According to the stories from managers who received the third degree in those sessions, these meetings were akin to picking a carcass clean. No element of financial performance was left untouched. Geneen was very successful for some time.

An accountant by training, Geneen believed that accounting numbers told all and that by examining the numbers it was possible to understand the substance of any business. He had 250 different businesses reporting to him, and Wall Street was singing his praises. Geneen believed the key to running diversified businesses was a thorough understanding of business results and that by having such an understanding, it was possible to compare the results of one operating unit with other units and determine where the company's resources should be deployed. His style of results management was subsequently adopted by many other companies.

Nonfinancial measures of performance are difficult for companies like ITT to comprehend because these measures of performance can significantly differ between the businesses. The way to measure the operating performance of a hotel such as Sheraton is very different than the way to measure operating performance in a property casualty insurance company such as Hartford Insurance.

The reality of the business was more complex than a single measure would capture. During the early 1970s, ITT suffered from overdiversification and found their businesses had little in common. In 1979, ITT began to divest the acquisitions; eventually, most of the acquisitions were divested, closed, or sold. Figure 7–4 shows the value of $100 invested in ITT from 1970 to 1990. After the major divestiture program began in earnest and ITT began to focus on a core business, the market responded and ITT's share values increased dramatically.

Geneen's specific techniques may have been discredited, but vestiges of the ideas remain in many of the performance-measurement systems in use today. Many companies are still using accounting measures of performance to measure results and by doing so are risking poor decision making on the part of their managers.

Accounting measures simply don't tell the whole story. Take as another example Waste Management and the aggressive expansion of that company from $4.5 billion in

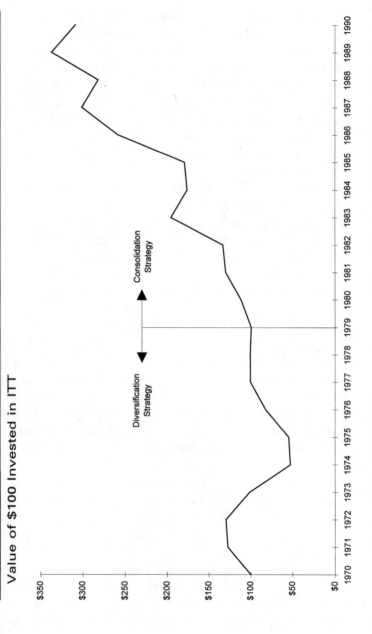

FIGURE 7-4

Value of $100 Invested in ITT

sales in 1989 to $8.7 billion in sales over four years. At the same time, earnings also grew quickly, from $1.22 to $1.86 per share. But the accounting numbers failed to tell the whole story. Although the industry was consolidating, the earnings growth was coming in part from expanding too quickly and not maintaining an adequate return on capital. The growth was not sustainable and certainly not at the historical level of return for capital. Investors looked beyond the accounting numbers and saw the diminishing prospects of the industry. Figure 7–5 shows the valuation of Waste Management based on a discounted future cash flow model and how the valuation changed compared to stock market pricing by investors, reflecting the shift in priorities of a changing industry.

Accounting is only part of the story. The shortcomings of the accounting measures are not an indictment of accounting but rather indicate the need to go beyond accounting to capture the financial and strategic performance of the company.

MYTH 3: YOU CAN MANAGE WITH FINANCIAL REPORTING

Two natural misconceptions support this myth. The first is the confusion and complexity of financial reporting, and the second is the success of the financially managed organizations. Financial reporting and financial performance measures are often so complex that they leave most operating managers scratching their heads. The language of financial results is different from the language of operations. Financial managers talk in terms of return on capital and leveraging assets. They refer to results in terms of NOPAT (net operating profit after tax) and EBITDA (earnings before interest, taxes, depreciation, and amortization). Because these terms are foreign to the average operating manager, the operating manager is happy to defer to the financial

FIGURE 7-5

Waste Management Market to Book Ratio

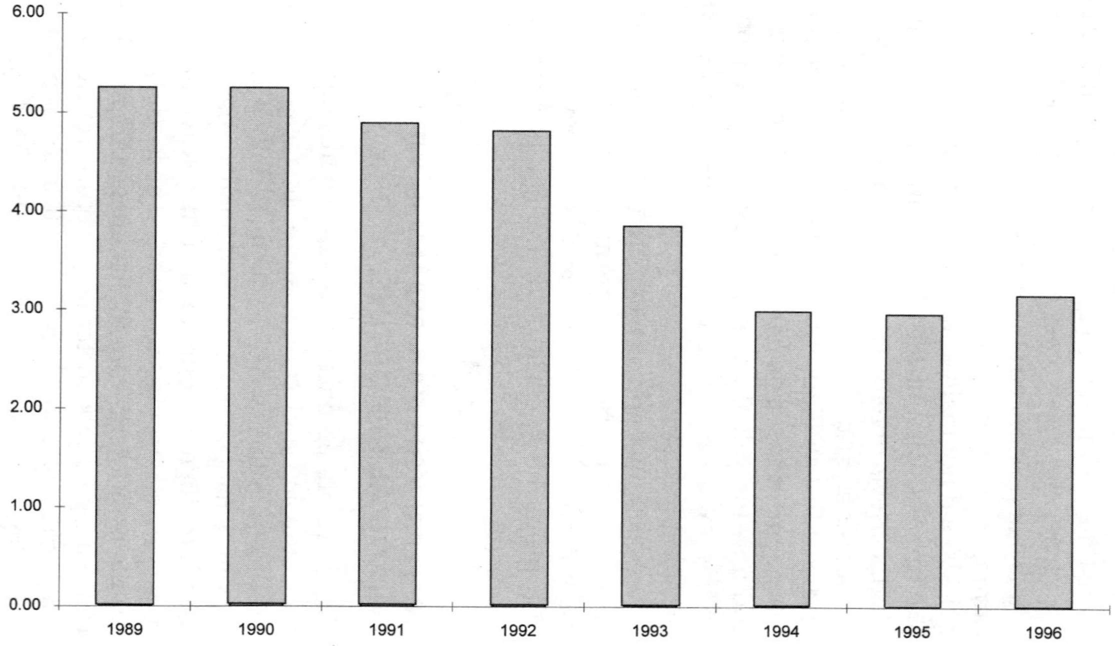

manager when it comes time to adopt or change the financial reporting measures and system.

Financial reporting is only one reporting system in a company. The primary job of financial reporting is to capture the company's financial results. The second reporting system in a company is the managerial reporting system. The primary job of managerial reporting is to provide operating management with the information they need to make informed decisions. If operating managers defer to financial managers to construct their managerial reporting systems, managerial reporting will end up being very similar to financial reporting. The other reason managerial reporting usually contains a strong dose of financial reporting language is the difficulty of developing and implementing nonfinancial operating performance measures.

Managing a company using financial reporting alone is like trying to drive a car by looking through the rearview mirror; results can be misleading and potentially dangerous. As long as you are driving in a straight line, the past is a decent indicator of the future. But as the road changes, past results can provide the wrong answers. For proof, look at IBM, where management for many years maintained the dogged determination that mainframe computers were the source of the company's competitive advantage. IBM management had good reason to put their faith in the supremacy of mainframes. After all, IBM's past success was defined by mainframes; successive generations of management had learned the business from prior generations that owed their success to mainframe technology.

Unfortunately, change comes to many industries. The change that swept the computer industry in the past 20 years was no less profound. The traditional mainframe and minicomputer vendors (IBM, Digital, and so on) watched as their business declined in the face of the onslaught of workstation and desktop computer manufacturers (Sun, Compaq, and so on).

Managers have been educated to manage by results, and the evidence of the effectiveness of this education surrounds us on the business landscape. Quarterly results, management by objectives, and hitting targets are just a few of the many terms designed to focus management on results. There is nothing wrong with managing for results, but be careful what you ask for.

Performance measures are helpful in managing the business when they accurately capture the issues influencing the decisions that managers are being asked to make. For example, if a hotel manager is asked to increase the return on assets and at the same time to improve the quality of service to the guests, the financial performance measure can easily conflict with the measure of quality service. Service quality may demand upgrading staff with training or different capabilities to provide better service to the customers, while the financial performance measure will suggest staff layoffs as a way to reduce head count and employee expense. Which is the right approach? It depends on your perspective. But regardless of which approach is correct, having two conflicting measures will send contradictory signals that will confuse and potentially paralyze the manager into inaction.

THE OPTIONS FOR MEASURING FINANCIAL PERFORMANCE

Financial performance measures can be very confusing to operating managers, leaving them asking, "How can we choose between return measures and quarterly income results?" There are numerous ways to measure financial performance, which can be logically grouped into four categories. Each category is related to and builds on the preceding categories:

1. Income.
2. Cash.

3. Return.

4. Value.

Tables 7–1(a) and 7–1(b) show the range of financial performance measures and define each one.

Income measures include operating profit (pre- and after tax), earnings before interest and taxes (EBIT), net income, and earnings per share. They are designed to measure the income generated by the company during a single period's operations. The differences between the measures lie in the information included in calculating them. For example, the operating profit of Monsanto in 1995 was different than the net income and earnings per share. In 1995, Monsanto had operating profit of $1.7 billion, EBIT of $1.2 billion, net income of $739 million, and earnings per share of $6.39. Table 7–2(a) is Monsanto's 1995 income statement; Table 7–2(b) identifies key performance measures.

The next category of financial performance measures is cash. Cash measures, like income measures, are designed to measure the operating results of a single period. The difference between cash and income measures is that cash measures capture the noncash charges in addition to the income. The cash-based financial performance measures most typically used are gross cash flow and EBITDA. Noncash charges to income, including depreciation, deferred taxes, and amortization, have no effect on the company's cash position. To measure the cash flow of the company in a single period, we can add back these noncash charges. Table 7–3 provides these cash-flow measures using Monsanto's 1995 results.

The third category of financial performance measures is the return measures. These measures come in many different shapes and sizes. They build off the income and cash-flow measures and add the dimension of return on the resources required to generate the income or cash flow. Return measures in common use today include: return on sales (ROS),

T A B L E 7-1(a)

Definitions of Profitability Measures

Profitability Measures

Measure	EBITDA (earnings before interest, taxes, depreciation, and amortization)	EBIT (earnings before interest and taxes)	NOPAT* (net operating profit after taxes)	Net Income	EPS (earnings per share)
Income statement	revenues − expenses <u>EBITDA</u>	revenues − expenses <u>EBITDA</u> − depreciation − amortization <u>EBIT</u>	revenues − expenses <u>EBITDA</u> − depreciation − amortization <u>EBIT</u> *(1 − tax rate) <u>NOPAT*</u>	revenues − expenses <u>EBITDA</u> − depreciation − amortization <u>EBIT</u> + interest income − interest expense *(1 − tax rate) <u>Net Income</u>	revenues − expenses <u>EBITDA</u> − depreciation − amortization <u>EBIT</u> + interest income − interest expense *(1 − tax rate) Net income Net income/ # shares outstanding <u>EPS</u>
Calculations					

*NOPAT excludes nonoperating income and expense.

T A B L E 7-1(b)

Definitions of Return and Single Period Value Added Measures

	Return Measures			Single Period $ Value Added	
Measure	ROE (return on equity)	RONA/ROCE (return on net assets)/ (return on capital employed)	ROGA (return on gross assets)	Economic value added	CVA (cash value added)
Income statement	revenues − expenses EBITDA − depreciation − amortization EBIT + interest income − interest expense *(1 − tax rate) Net income	revenues − expenses EBITDA − depreciation − amortization EBIT *(1 − tax rate) NOPAT*	revenues − expenses EBITDA − depreciation − amortization EBIT *(1 − tax rate) NOPAT* + depreciation GOPAT**	revenues − expenses EBITDA − depreciation − amortization EBIT *(1 − tax rate) NOPAT*	revenues − expenses EBITDA − depreciation − amortization EBIT *(1 − tax rate) NOPAT* + depreciation GOPAT**
Balance sheet	total common equity	total assets − noninterest-bearing current liabilities Net assets	total assets − noninterest-bearing current liabilities + accumulated depreciation Gross assets	total assets − noninterest-bearing current liabilities Net assets	total assets − noninterest-bearing current liabilities + accumulated depreciation Gross assets
Calculation	Net income/ total common equity ROE	NOPAT/ Net assets RONA/ROC	GOPAT**/ Gross assets ROGA	NOPAT − (cost of capital *Net assets) Economic value added	GOPAT** − (Cost of capital * gross assets) CVA

*NOPAT (Net Operating Profit After Taxes) excludes nonoperating income and expense.

**GOPAT (Gross Operating Profit After Taxes) equals NOPAT + depreciation.

191

TABLE 7–2(a)

Monsanto 1995 Income Statement
($ millions)

Net Sales	8,962
COGS	(5,109)
Gross Profit	3,853
Marketing expense	(1,282)
Administrative expense	(598)
Technological expense	(713)
Amortization of intangible assets	(119)
Restructuring and other special charges — net	(156)
Operating income	985
Interest expense	(190)
Interest income	59
Gain on sale of business	189
Other income (expense) — net	44
Pretax income	1,087
Income taxes	(348)
Net income	739
Earnings per share	1.27
EBIT	1,218

return on equity (ROE), return on assets (ROA), return on capital (ROC), return on capital employed (ROCE), return on net assets (RONA), return on gross assets (ROGA), return on gross investment (ROGI), and cash flow return on investment (CFROI). These return measures do not measure return on the same basis. Some measure return based on sales, others on equity, and still others on assets. When measuring returns on assets, there is no single definition of what constitutes the asset base. An asset base may include all assets. An alterna-

T A B L E 7-2(b)

Interpretation of Key Performance Measures

Performance Measure	Calculation of Measure	Information Conveyed
Operating profit (pretax or after tax)	Net sales − cost of goods sold − operating expenses (e.g., selling, general, & administrative expense)	The measure only takes into account operating activities and excludes all nonreoccuring and financing activities. Focuses the individual on only improving the operational side of the business.
Earnings before interest and taxes	Net sales + other income − cost of goods sold − all expenses except interest expense − minority expense	The measure not only takes into account all operating activities but also one time events. Financing activities and taxes are excluded. Focuses the individual on improving pretax, prefinance earnings by increasing all aspects of income and expense including non cash and restructuring charges.
Earnings after taxes	Net sales + other income − cost of goods sold − all expenses − income tax − minority expense	The measure takes into account all operating and financing activities and taxes. Focuses the individual on both the operating and financing sides of the business.
Net income	Net sales + other income − cost of goods sold − all expenses − income tax − minority expense − extraordinary and discontinued items	In addition to operating and financing activities, the income or loss from discontinued operations and extraordinary items (infrequent and unusual events) are taken into account. Focuses the individual on every aspect of the business, and income can be increased or decreased through many avenues besides the normal operating activities of the business.
Earnings per share	(Net income − preferred dividends)/ average common shares outstanding	Net income is translated into a per share basis.

T A B L E   7–3

Monsanto 1995 Cash
Results (millions)

EBIT	$1,218
Gross Cash Flow	$823
EBITDA	$1,796

tive approach subtracts the noninterest-bearing current liabilities from the stated assets to determine the adjusted asset
base. In addition, each company that uses a measure of return
usually has a special twist in the definition of the assets that
is peculiar to that company.

The fourth category of financial performance measures
is value. Value is expressed as either a period measure or
a measure at a point in time of multiple periods that defines
the worth of the business. Typical period measures of value
include: economic value added (EVA),[5] economic profit
(EP), shareholder value added (SVA), and cash value added
(CVA). Economic value added, economic profit and shareholder value added are actually identical measures. Economic value added is primarily based on earnings where
cash value added is based on cash.

Measures of value at a point in time include: stock
price, net present value (NPV), market value added (MVA)
cash flow multiples, and cash flow simulation techniques
such as spot value,[6] plan value,[7] and discounted cash flow
simulation (DCFS).[8] In each case, the point-in-time value
measure is compared to a previous or future point in time
to determine the amount of value that has been or is expected to be created during the forecast time horizon. For
example, if the value is $1,000 in the present period and
$900 in the prior period, we can say that value has increased
$100 in the present period and that investors received a

$100 return on a $900 investment. Let's look at an example of the application of these value-based measures to a company. Figure 7–6 illustrates the convergence of the actual versus predicted stock price using the DCFS method from 1987–1996 for Monsanto. We see that Monsanto's stock price range reflects the economics as measured by DCFS.

CHOOSING PERFORMANCE MEASURES

Choosing which of these measures is right for your company is an important activity that can make an enormous difference in the way decisions are made. Historically, financial performance measures were chosen either because they had previously been used or based on personal preference. These are not the best ways to select a measurement system.

The alternative is a structured approach that captures all the issues the company wants to include in the measure and focuses on maximizing the value of the measure to the organization.

Following a structured approach to performance measurement has large payoffs. A structured approach increases the likelihood that the measurement system will succeed by providing the desired behavioral signals to support good decision making. Construction and implementation of a structured process requires understanding six related issues: accuracy, complexity, correlation, industry fit, company fit, and strategy fit (see Figure 7–7).

When analyzed together, these six issues encompass a thorough review of the existing performance measures, offering the opportunity to fully evaluate the implications of different measures and the signals they provide for managerial decision making.

Accuracy

Accuracy is the issue of how well the measure captures the fundamental economics of the business. Rarely will a single

FIGURE 7-6

Monsanto Actual vs. Predicted Stock Price DCFS Model

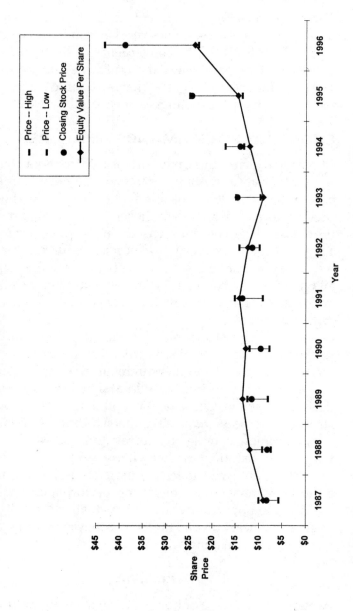

FIGURE 7-7

A Structural Approach to Performance Measurement Selection is Critical to an Effective Decision-Making Process

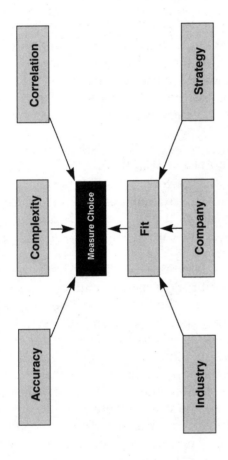

It facilitates understanding of economic factors and prioritizes management's focus

From James Knight, "Performance Measures and Strategy," *Handbook of Business Strategy*, 1996 edition, Chicago: Faulkner and Gray, 1996. Printed with permission.

measure capture all the economics. More likely, a single measure will serve as shorthand to communicate the important economic issues. For example, in the real estate business, the old maxim is location, location, location. Location is actually a shorthand definition underscoring the importance of the economics affecting the real estate business. The concept of location explains that the value to be derived from a property lies in that property's ability to generate sufficient cash flows to be attractive as an investment opportunity. Cash flows are in turn driven by the tenant's desire for the property, the premise being that the more attractive the location, the higher a premium the tenant will pay for the property.

Is this always true? No. There are many examples that disprove the rule of location as the only determinant of value in real estate. Other factors, including population density, accessibility, and supply and demand, all figure into the economic proposition. If one measure is not enough, how good does a single measure need to be? Or should you use multiple measures?

One way to determine whether a single measure will suffice or if multiple measures will be more effective involves determining the accuracy of the proposed measures. This process begins with an understanding of the important business issues. For example, if there are many noncash charges in the course of operating the business, including cash as opposed to income may make sense. If a business is capital intensive, a return measure may make more sense than an income measure because the return measure can capture the returns on the capital invested in the business. Value measures may make sense when the business confronts the difficulties of balancing growth and profitability. Focusing on return measures alone may tend to discourage growth by solely emphasizing profitability improvement. This may not be the best signal when the business is highly profitable but needs to grow. When accuracy is required across multiple time periods, including strategic measures can make a lot of sense. Strategic measures become important when business issues do not lend themselves to single-period financial-performance measures. Examples include R&D expenditures, advertising to create brand identity and awareness, and other investments and expenses. Although these expenditures may be made in a single period, the company may not realize the benefit of the investment until some time in the future.

Take the example of GD Searle, a unit of Monsanto, that was widely criticized for not developing a new drug research and application pipeline. Then they discovered that one of their chemical compounds could be used in the treatment of arthritis. Single-period performance measures did not capture the potential value of these new compounds. Yet Searle's measures of performance were very accurate. Like most things, accuracy comes at a price, and the price is called complexity.

Complexity

Complexity can be thought of in two ways:

1. The company's difficulty in assembling the information required to calculate the measure.
2. The operating manager's ability to use the measure.

A measure is only as good as the information it contains and the willingness of the management team to use it. If the measure requires information to be calculated that is not readily available, the problem of calculating the measure may dwarf any potential benefit of increasing the accuracy. The availability or absence of division-level asset information needed for use in calculating some type of return measure provides one such example. If the unit does not keep balance sheets, the information may not be readily available. This roadblock to calculating the measure then requires alternate systems to capture the information or use of a simpler measure.

The other complexity issue relates to the operating managers' purpose in using the measure for decision making. Here the question lies in the intended use of the measure. If the measure is difficult to calculate, the manager is not likely to use it for decision making. An unused performance measure adds little value. In order to assess an operating manager's use of the measure, we will put the measure through a "windshield test." Can the operating manager, while driving home with both hands on the steering wheel and both eyes looking straight ahead through the windshield, calculate the performance measure? If the answer is no, the measure fails the windshield test.

In fairness, some education is required to implement any new measure, but the end result must be a passing score on the windshield test. If the measure does not pass the test, ultimately the performance measure will not be used. Instead, it will be relegated to the back room where financial managers with green eyeshades will continue calculating it, only providing the results to the operating managers at some distant date in the future. These back-room measures do not work well because in cases where there is limited understanding there is also limited ability to infer the implications of the measure's results and little or no practical use of the measure. This significantly reduces the value of the measure as a management decision-making tool.

There is usually a trade-off between accuracy and complexity. The higher the accuracy, the more complexity; the lower the accuracy, the less complexity. The trick is to balance the need for accuracy with the availability of information and the organization's appetite for complexity. Figure 7–8 illustrates the accuracy/complexity trade-off for a number of well-known financial measures.

There is an interesting point to be made here about accuracy and complexity and the different types of measures, whether they be income, cash, return, or value measures. The common perception is that the measures of income, cash, return, and value are different, but in reality they are not. Every measure can be reconciled to every other measure to any number of significant digits you choose. You can move from one measure to the next simply by adding more information. The more information you add, the more complex the measure but also the more accurate the measure. Returning to Figure 7–8, it is then easy to see that the opportunities for reconciling the measures also provide opportunities to customize the measures to capture the economics of the business by adding more information. We are no longer bound by the individual measures discussed above but can customize a measure for our own use. The measures above are simply a starting point in the process of developing the measure or measures that are right for the organization.

Proponents of individual measures also describe how to customize those measures. For example, at last count there were 162 possible adjustments you can make to economic value added. If you make all the adjustments, you end up with a modified version of cash flow return on investment (CFROI). The measure is just a starting point. The real art of selecting appropriate performance measures requires careful identification of the business issues that need to be included so the measure is robust. The measure should explain the economics of the business while remaining simple enough to be used in operating decision making. After all, it is pointless to make the operating managers into finance experts just so they can use the measures.

FIGURE 7-8

Economic Value Added and CFROI Can Be Reconciled—The Measure is Just a Tool

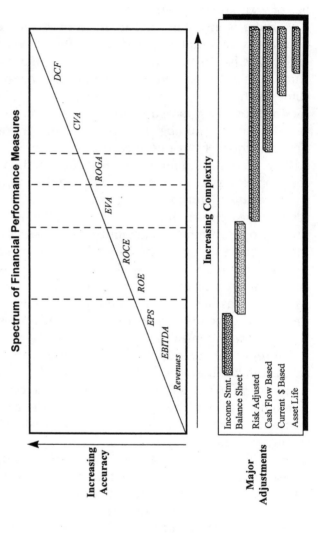

Spectrum of Financial Performance Measures

Increasing Accuracy

Revenues
EBITDA
EPS
ROE
ROCE
EVA
ROGA
CVA
DCF

Increasing Complexity

Major Adjustments

Income Stmt.
Balance Sheet
Risk Adjusted
Cash Flow Based
Current $ Based
Asset Life

Correlation

The interest of shareholders must be the focus of any performance-measurement system. The success of a performance-measurement system at tracking and consistently reflecting shareholders' interests demonstrates how well it achieves this objective. One example of why correlation makes a difference can be seen in the highly profitable company that uses a return measure as the yardstick to judge its performance. The return measure motivates management to achieve higher returns. However, the interests of the shareholders may be better served through a combination of obtaining higher returns while investing in growth opportunities.

To illustrate this phenomena of maximizing returns at the expense of the shareholders, let's return to our friends at Apple Computer in the early 1990s, as shown in Figure 7–9. In 1990, Apple had high returns measured by return on net assets (RONA).

At that time, management used a hurdle rate of 30 percent to evaluate new investments. Because the number of projects that exceeded the hurdle rate were few and far between, Apple accumulated a large store of cash, as shown in Figure 7–10.

The cash was earning 3 percent at best after tax, yet Apple was turning down projects with internal rates of return above 20 percent. Twenty percent returns are comparable to the returns of the more profitable pharmaceutical companies, exceed the returns of most branded consumer goods companies, and rank well within the top 10 percent of overall business returns. At the same time, the computer industry was becoming more and more competitive, placing additional emphasis on cost position. Apple stuck with the strategy of selling at a premium price, while foregoing the opportunity to reinvest the cash and compete for market share. The result of this series

204

Apple Computer, S&P 500 Median, and Industry Peer Group Median
1990 Return on Net Assets

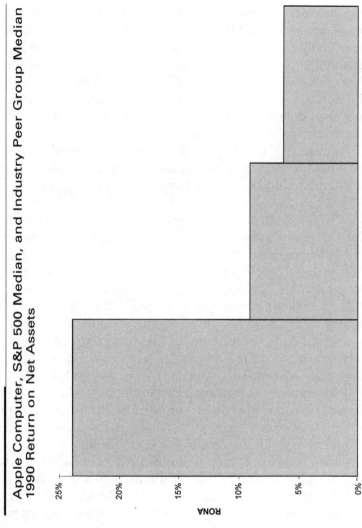

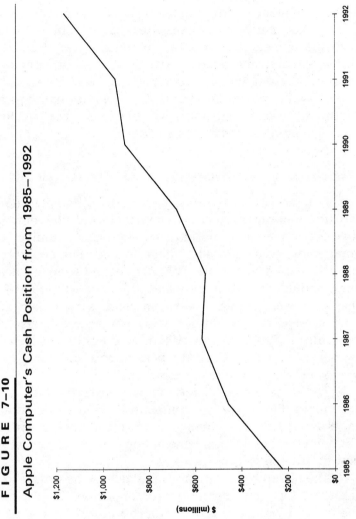

FIGURE 7–10

Apple Computer's Cash Position from 1985–1992

of poor decisions drove Apple to the brink. Apple's shareholders wanted a combination of returns and growth, while management emphasized returns. The moral of the story is that performance measures that are out of synch with the owners' interests can in times of rapid change cost the company dearly. Analyzing the performance measure(s) from the standpoint of the shareholder is a necessary ingredient in developing a performance-measurement system that addresses the long-term, wealth-creating interests of the shareholders.

Industry, Company, and Strategy Fit

Different industries, of course, have vastly different characteristics. Some important characteristics include the competitive economic situation, industry economics, number of competitors, asset intensity, intellectual content, and product life cycle. A combination of financial and strategic measures should address these issues of industry fit to ensure that the selected performance measure serves management's purpose. If the industry is expanding, as the personal computer industry was in 1990, it becomes especially important to make sure that the performance measures you are using track the industry dynamics.

The same is true for the company, except in this case we will want to analyze the company's culture to determine the effective implementation of performance measurement. Different recipes for implementation and adoption work best in different settings.

The hierarchical company legislates the new measures from the top or center of the organization. The rest of the company then falls into line by accepting the new measure as the measure of choice and tying large percentages of the incentive payments to the measure. There are fewer and fewer of these hierarchical companies today, but those that exist can change performance measurement systems more easily than those that require or desire a more collaborative approach to the adoption of the performance measures.

Other companies with a more collaborative style of management will be better served by proceeding more slowly when adopting new performance-measure systems. Newspaper companies are usually very consensus driven, and the ones that have tried to alter their performance measures from the center of the organization without the buy-in of the rest of the organization have found themselves redoing the performance measures in a short period of time because the organization pushes back against the change and refuses to adopt the new system.

Performance measurement systems must be linked to the business strategy to be truly successful in helping managers make better decisions. The business strategy should drive decision making, and the performance measure should reinforce the strategy by sending the correct signals to managers regarding the objectives of their decision-making and resource allocation. When the business strategy calls for growth while the performance measures focus on improved returns, the inherent conflict between the two messages will undermine the effectiveness of the business strategy. The company may achieve improved returns, but they will come at the expense of growth.

TRADE-OFFS

The selection, implementation, and use of a performance measure requires evaluating a series of trade-offs that involve the company, its industry, and consideration of the company's strategy from multiple perspectives. The selected performance measures should provide managers in the organization with guidance and support for good decision making. The following are some of the trade-offs that most often require careful thought and consideration:

- Financial/strategic objectives.
- Single/multiple period time frame.
- Activity/result orientation.

Selecting performance measures requires examining the possible financial and strategic measures that can capture all or most of the key business issues.

Results will always be important, and measuring the results correctly is an important objective for any performance-measurement system. Successful performance systems require a considered approach to designing the measurement system. In the process, you will want to identify which financial performance measures are right for your company and customize them as necessary. You may need to augment the financial measures with additional strategic measures to better capture the decisions in the business.

OPTIONS FOR STRATEGIC PERFORMANCE

As we have discussed, financial performance tells only part of the story. To complete the story, we need to consider strategic performance measures. Strategic performance measures include the decisions that are right for the business, but the results of these decisions may not show up in the financial performance results in a single period. Strategic performance measures differ from industry to industry and from company to company. Strategic performance measures should include customer relationships, employee relationships, and capability enhancement. Some companies refer to these strategic performance measures as the "balanced scorecard."[9] Figure 7–11 is an example of a balanced scorecard of strategic performance measures.

The process for developing the strategic measures is

Single Period Financial Measures Only Tell Part of the Story

Balanced Scorecard

Financial	Customer
• Profitability (Short and Long-term) • Long-term Value Creation	• Right Customer • Provide Solutions
Product	**Infrastructure**
• Right Products	• Provide Solutions • Teamwork/Cross Selling • Seamless Process

Critical Success Factors

Performance Measures

Expectations/Targets

often as important as the measures themselves. When done correctly, the strategic-measure development process can add substantially to the communication and shared understanding of the organization about the importance and relative priorities of different programs and activities across businesses and functions while providing a context for decision making.

The decision of how to balance and trade off the financial and strategic results is primarily an issue of how quickly the results will show themselves. Financial results show up in a single period. The benefits of strategic measures may not show up until future periods. When used correctly, strategic measures can help balance the signals for managers, but they also can be used as a cloak for poor decision making. One example of successfully integrating financial and strategic measures is the case of a bank that was interested in focusing their loan officers on driving new business while at the same time building the long-term relationship of the bank with the customer. They wanted to recognize that the true value of the customer extends well beyond a single measurement period. The bank wanted to encourage calling officers to do the right thing for the long-term value of the customer to the bank, while at the same time they recognized that such a decision to do the right thing for the long term might penalize the calling officer in a single financial-performance period. To accomplish its goal, the bank chose a combination of financial and strategic measures in a balanced scorecard-type format to focus the calling officers on both driving performance in the single financial reporting period and potential long-term customer value to the bank.

The distinction between financial and strategic measures is similar to but different than the distinction between single- and multiple-period measurement. One of the important issues in single-period performance measurement is the lagging doubt about sustainable performance. Using a combination of single- and multiple-period measures can help focus management not only on the period's results but also on the sustainability of the results. Single-period measures leave the door open to spikes in performance that in reality are not sustainable.

Three common ways to deal with the challenge of sustainable results are measures, averaging, and cumulative measurement. Averaging takes the performance over multiple periods and averages it. The cumulative concept makes good performance an additive and the bad performance a subtraction. This concept is often translated into banking in compensation. This design is discussed in greater detail in Chapter 8 within the context of incentive plans.

One of the oldest debates in performance measures is the question of activity or results. Many on Wall Street would argue that results are all that matters. Others, like W. Edwards Deming (the deceased dean of the quality movement), suggest that activities should be measured and that the results will naturally follow suit. Like most things, the truth probably lies somewhere in the middle. It is beguiling to consider solely measuring activities and taking the view that if you do the right things, the desired results will be achieved. Unfortunately, western capitalism is more demanding and short-term oriented. Investors, sometimes impatient, expect quick results for the activity invested. The argument is probably unwinnable on either side. But what does make sense in either case is to make sure the activities and results are linked through the performance-measurement system.

No results-driven system can be perfect. Performance measures can and should encourage the right activities to achieve the desired results. The challenge is helping people understand how they can influence the results through the activities they undertake.

Choosing the performance measures in a structured process is an important implementation step in and of itself.

There are seven simple questions you can use to ensure that you have considered both the important elements in selecting a performance measure(s) and the trade-offs:

1. What are the important business economics?
2. What adjustments are necessary and why?
3. Do we capture the strategy issues that will not show up in a single period?
4. How are financial measures correlated to value?
5. What is the appropriate time horizon?
6. What information is available?
7. What are the pros/cons from a fit perspective?

In addition to these seven questions, make certain the performance you are measuring is meaningful and manageable. If it is meaningful but not manageable, the problem lies not with the performance measurement but elsewhere. If the performance is manageable but not meaningful, it does not make sense to include the performance measure in the decision making of the company. If you use too many measures, you will dilute the focus. Figure 7–12 shows two attributes that help prioritize the measures.

Performance measures are an important tool for management and when appropriately selected and implemented can help drive value-creating behavior. The choice of the performance measure sets the stage for decision making in the company. When appropriately chosen, performance measures can provide valuable information for management decision making. Striking the right balance between single-period financial results and decisions where the results take longer is an important opportunity to improve managerial decision making and focus managers on what is important to strategy execution.

F I G U R E   7–12

Importance of Including Performance Measures in Decision Making

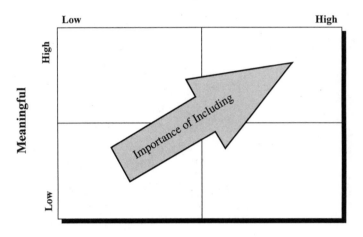

CHAPTER 8

Compensation Strategy

There is currently a serious lack of original thought in the area of incentive compensation. It is typically viewed as a tool for motivation and pay delivery. In most companies, the compensation lacks a coherent strategy and is based more on a bell-curve style grading of employees than anything else. Incentive compensation programs primarily relate to compensation delivery and have little, if anything, to do with business strategy. Thus, today's compensation programs are generally designed to be competitive with peer companies within the industry. Although well-intentioned, these beliefs miss the real point of incentive compensation, which is to focus management on achieving the business strategy.

Incentive plans within industries are much the same from one company to the next. For example, let us compare AT&T's incentive plan to the plans of other long-distance telecommunication providers. Table 8–1 illustrates the similarity.

The compensation plans in long-distance companies are the same because they are designed as a separate activity

TABLE 8-1

Long-Distance Companies' Pay Comparison

	AT&T	MCI	Sprint
Philosophy	Compensation level at the 50th-60th percentile of its peer group	Compensation level at the 50th-75th percentile of its peer group	Compensation level at the 50th-75th percentile of its peer group
Annual incentive	Based on value measures	Based on profitability and strategic measures	Based on value and profitability measures
Stock options	Time vesting	Time vesting	Time vesting
Restricted Stock (RS)	No RS	No RS	No RS
Long-Term Incentive Plan (LTIP)	Three-year rolling plan based on a return measure	No LTIP	Three-year rolling plan based on a return and profitability measure

Source: SCA proxy analysis.

removed from the business strategy. These plans live on from year to year with minor revisions that address competitiveness of pay but do little to support the business strategy. The extent of the typical revision is usually to alter the salary ranges or modify the bonus opportunity. Is it any surprise these copycat programs lead to mediocre results? If you look at AT&T's plan three years ago and compare it with the current plan, you will find little change.

This tyranny of mediocrity creates three real problems for companies:

1. Compensation does not support the business strategy.
2. Excellent performance is worth little more than average performance.
3. Pay packages are designed as one-size-fits-all.

Incentives that do not support business strategy are the greatest unseen problem in compensation today. Compensation systems can be the single most destructive influence on strategy execution. This lack of an apparent connection to the business strategy means the company is foregoing the opportunity to use pay as a way to focus employees on the results the company is trying to achieve.

The cost of this lack of focus is potentially enormous. Take the S&P 400 Industrials as a group that employs 11.3 million people and use a very conservative estimate of $50,000 per person as the employees' cost including salary and incentives. Using these assumptions, we can estimate the cost of compensation in the S&P 400 as $565 billion. The opportunity to improve the return on the compensation expense is enormous. If we saw only a 1 percent increase in productivity from improved decision making, and studies suggest the potential could be 10 times as much as a result of improved compensation plans that better supported the company's strategy, we would be talking about improving

profits by $11 billion! The stakes are huge, and the opportu-
nity is unexplored.

Companies are not offering substantially better incentive compensation opportunities to their excellent employees. This is unfortunate because labor is a large portion of
the value added in companies, yet the opportunity to use
incentive compensation to encourage performance is going
largely ignored. Is it any wonder that star performers are
attracted to smaller more entrepreneurial companies that
will recognize their contribution?

The one-size-fits-all approach to compensation design
assumes that all participants value the pay elements equally.
Figure 8–1 illustrates how a single design can be interpreted
differently by different people.

Different people have different needs and can attach
vastly different values to pay-package elements. A one-size-

FIGURE 8-1

Person A is Highly Risk Adverse; Person B is Risk
Neutral; and Person C is a Risk Taker

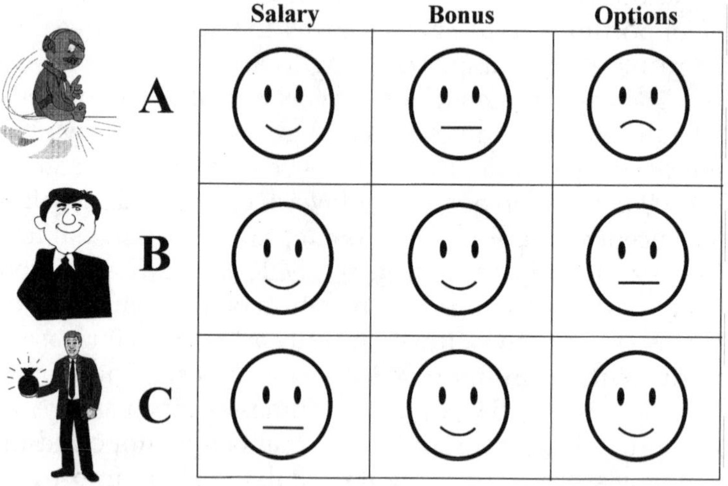

fits-all design does nothing to respond to the individual needs of the employees and misses the opportunity to construct categories or pay-package differentiation by group that better meet the needs of both the company and the employee.

EQUAL RESULTS

In today's incentive compensation plans, bonus ranges, restricted stock, and stock option grants are often based on job grade. Managers receive incentives because of their positions, not their performance. Compensation incentives are designed based on prior compensation plans with a focus on minimizing the difference between individuals within classes or groups in the name of equitable treatment. This is the wrong way to think about incentives. Incentive compensation programs should be designed to provide equal *opportunity*, not necessarily to guarantee equal results. Equal results remove the true incentive opportunity and reduce the focus on performance. Ironically, the further down you look in the organization, the more pronounced the problem becomes because the participation is smaller and the percentage of variable pay relative to total pay based on performance is reduced.

There are some compelling reasons to increase variable pay. Studies have shown that it boosts productivity. If properly implemented, greater use of variable pay reduces the chances of layoffs in downturns and decreases employment by lowering the marginal cost of an additional worker. However, according to the *Economist,* only 12 percent of workers in the United States participate in variable-pay programs. That rate is not much different in the United Kingdom or Germany.

Now lets examine CEO pay relative to CEO performance for shareholders. Figure 8–2 shows how CEOs performed for their shareholders compared to the compensa-

F I G U R E 8-2

Pay for Performance Relationship: CEO Total
Compensation vs. Total Shareholder Return
(1994-1996)

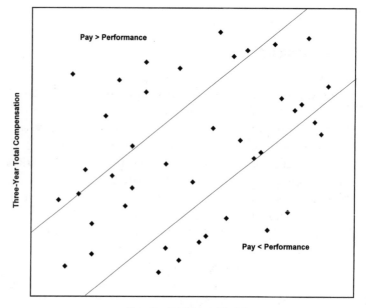

Source: SCA analysis.

tion they received. You'll notice in the data the absence of
a strong relationship between pay and performance. This
raises two issues:

1. Is the CEO's pay sufficiently tied to performance?
2. Is the range in CEO performance-based pay
   enough to reflect the differences in performance?

The lack of a spread in the incentives awarded creates a
problem because it indicates that regardless of how you
perform, there will be relatively little difference in the pay
you receive.

Another flaw in most incentives today is that they are not effectively tied to line-of-sight performance. Line-of-sight performance represents the decisions a manager makes or can affect. Stock-option-based performance is largely based on changes driven by the stock market and has little to do with operating decisions. Managers are left with no clear link between what they do and the results that determine their pay. This leads to confusion on the part of the individual's supervisor. How is the supervisor supposed to determine the individual incentive payments and make distinctions between the performance of individuals in his or her group if the actual payment is based on factors outside the individual's control? And what if the basis for dividing incentives is subjective?

Often the guidelines are either unclear or highly subjective. This places the supervisor in a terrible position because he or she must explain the incentive award and the basis for its calculation to each individual and justify any inequities with others. If the determination of the award is subjective, it is much easier for the supervisor if he or she minimizes the spread in the award paid to different individuals.

Think about the process of determining the incentive award. The supervisor determines an award to recognize the individual's contribution. Yet the supervisor knows that if there is too much variation in the incentive awards paid to all individuals, the person being reviewed will respond in one of the following ways:

- Be displeased and want to know why the variation was so great.
- Want to know why she or he was not at or close to the top of the range of awards.
- Just be unhappy with the award.

It is much easier for the boss to minimize the variation because a narrower range will reduce the level of displeasure.

Today's incentive program designs place too much emphasis on the monetary value of the incentive and not enough on its appropriateness. The majority of the time is spent defining the monetary value. Very little is spent matching the incentive to the decisions to be made, to the company's strategic direction, or to the link between performance and pay.

Today's typical compensation program is well intended but ineffective for the following reasons:

- It does not place enough emphasis on pay for performance.
- It confuses the opportunities with the results and ends up providing roughly equal amounts of pay for different performance.
- It has little if anything to do with the strategy beyond the perfunctory goal of "improve the profits."

Incentives are often ignored as a way to focus managers on the company's strategy by encouraging decisions that reinforce the strategy and improve the desired results.

Let's explore the example of Heavy Capital company. Heavy Capital is a real company in the Fortune 500. It is in a capital-intensive industry and is using a return on equity (ROE) measure as the basis for granting long-term stock option awards. The ROE must surpass a threshold of 20 percent for the payout of the long-term awards to the senior executives.

The company has traditionally earned 20 percent in good years and lost at least 5 percent in bad years. On the surface, the 20 percent goal for ROE appears to be a stretch but is not unreasonable in light of past performance (see Figure 8–3). If we dig a little deeper, we find that the company has a very old plant and until 1991, was not making the capital investments required to keep

Return on Equity for Heavy Capital (1976-1995)

pace with competitors in a rapidly changing marketplace (see Figure 8–4).

The company also lags behind the industry in the sheer scale of its business. Heavy equipment is one-third the size, as measured by revenue, of the largest company in the industry, and three other competitors are twice as large. The key to increasing the scale of the company is growing revenues, but the company's existing plants are already working at full capacity to meet the demand. Heavy Capital has delayed its capital investments for too long, and they now have a real need to measure capacity if they are going to be a longtime player in the industry.

Heavy Capital's incentive compensation program may be holding them back from making the investments required because it does not support the business strategy. In fact, it may actually be placing the business strategy at risk. While the business strategy requires renewal and growth, the incentives are focusing management behavior on improving profitability by focusing on ROE. Improving ROE discourages new investment. The older the existing investment, the greater the problem will become. The incentives are sending very strong signals to management not to reinvest in the business.

Table 8–2 gives a quick illustration of incentives from the viewpoint of one of the senior vice presidents who is running one of the facilities. It is not in the best interest of this senior executive to reinvest in the business, as we can clearly see from the illustration. If the executive reinvests in the business, it will increase the denominator of his ROE, so his ROE will decline relative to the same level of executive income. Even if he increases his income, his ROE will still decline because the existing plant is highly depreciated and the new investment will add disproportionately to the equity base of his plan.

There are real opportunities to improve Heavy Capital's incentive program:

Heavy Capital and Industry Peer Group Capital Expenditures as a Percent of Depreciation

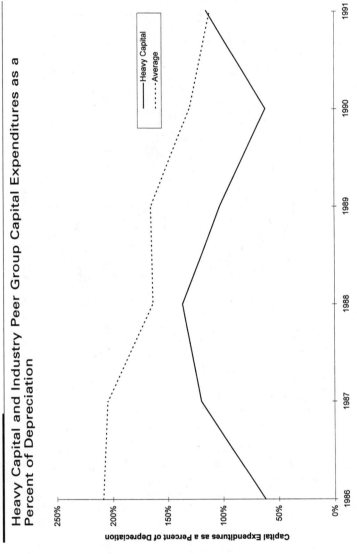

226

T A B L E 8-2

Comparison of Senior Vice President's Incentives With and Without Capital Investment

	Without Capital Investment	With Capital Investment
Asset base	Will decrease due to an increase in accumulated depreciation leading to an increase in RONA.*	Will increase causing in RONA* to decrease.
Depreciation expense	Remains constant and RONA* also remains the same.	Will increase due to the new capital investments leading to a decrease in earnings causing in RONA* to decrease.
RONA measure	Will not be affected since no new assets were added.	The new asset will have a lower RONA* than the existing asset due to lower accumulated depreciation on that asset, resulting in a larger asset base.
Example	$20 million operating profit / $100 million capital base RONA* = 20%	$20 million operating profit / ($20 million additional investment + $100 million capital base) RONA* = 16.7%

*Return on Net Assets = Net Operating Profit after Taxes/(Total Assets − Non-Interest Bearing Current Liabilities).

- Today's short-term focus can be extended by modifying the incentive program to reflect a more balanced view going forward with equal emphasis on the short term and the long term.
- Today's emphasis on profitability can be modified to also emphasize growth in sales and provide relief to managers who make the right investments in the future growth of the business.
- The ROE measure can be replaced with or augmented by other measures that have a better line of sight for the operating managers in the business and can then be extended down into the organization to improve decision making.

FROM EQUAL RESULTS TO EQUAL OPPORTUNITY

The purpose of an incentive is to motivate the individual to perform and to reward the individual for that performance. How did incentives evolve from being focused on equal opportunity tied to performance to an orientation of equal results? Management must accept responsibility for this change in focus. It is management's job to distinguish between employees who are performing and those who are not. This means management has to assess performance. But management has resisted making the tough assessments of performance, instead minimizing the differences between employees who perform well and employees who perform poorly. Management's aversion to tough decisions has led to relatively flat incentive results in many companies.

This is a good news/bad news situation. The bad news is that these are serious problems that need to be addressed; the good news is that the opportunity that comes from addressing these problems is huge. We can look at the sheer magnitude of changes in the S&P 400 to understand how large an opportunity exists for improvement. Even a small improvement in productivity from more effective incentives offers a large opportunity to create value.

There is an alternative to "equal results": Focus on configuring the incentives to support the business strategy. The effective incentive system flows naturally from the business strategy and focuses on driving behavior that helps achieve the objectives of the business strategy. Figure 8–5 depicts the relationship between strategy, financial performance, and behavior.

Incentives have little meaning without the link to strategy. When linked to strategy, the incentives become part of the strategy's implementation. Focusing incentives and

FIGURE 8–5

Relationship Between Strategy, Finance, and Behavior

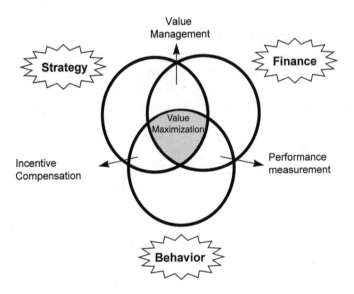

behavior is a powerful, but currently underused, tool that can help management achieve the company's strategic objectives.

Based on the principles described in Table 8–3, we can develop directional implications for compensation strategies.

To build the link between business strategy and incentive pay, you must first establish the link between strategy and performance measures, as described in Chapter 2. Only then can you begin developing the link between strategy and incentive pay using the performance measures to capture the results. A set of performance measures that correctly measures the strategy is an invaluable and necessary tool in an effective strategically driven compensation program.

Incentives become a powerful tool, focusing behavior to achieve strategic and financial results. Because no two companies have the same strategies, a general discussion will not be appropriate or useful. Instead, let's examine a hypothetical company, its strategy, performance measures, and incentives to see how they all work together.

Senior management will want to begin with an understanding of the principles for the compensation strategy. One example of how the principles can be applied is as follows:

1. Encourage innovative thinking and approaches to the business.

2. Reward contribution, not entitlement or seniority/tenure.

3. Encourage team-based behavior.

4. Provide line of sight to the team/individual.

5. Focus on value-based metrics.

6. Recognize how each business unit contributes to value.

T A B L E 8-3

Compensation Principles and Direction

Compensation Principles	Directional Implications
■ Encourage innovative thinking and approaches to the business and to pay	■ Nontraditional approaches to pay
	■ Flexible systems (respond to change)
■ Reward for contribution, not entitlement or seniority/tenure	■ Pay for the person, not the job
	■ Nonhierarchical base pay structures
	■ Performance-driven pay mix
■ Provide line of sight to the team/individual	■ Flexibility to fund/allocate incentives at the most appropriate level (Enterprise, Business Unit/country, business within Business Unit, working teams, individual)
■ Encourage team-based behavior	■ Explicitly reward integration contributions
■ Focus on value-based metrics	■ Performance measures that drive enterprise value (total shareholder return, EVA®/CFROI)
■ Build a leveraged pay system	■ Emphasis on variable pay elements
	- Extraordinary pay for extraordinary performance
	- Below-average pay for below-average performance
■ Build ownership mentality throughout the company (at the appropriate level)	■ Extension of variable pay throughout the organization (management incentives, team incentives, gain sharing, etc.)
	■ Aggressive use of equity (leveraged equity, phantom stock)
■ Develop an overall program with credibility and organization confidence	■ Simple and understandable
	■ Open communication
	■ Objective

7. Build an ownership mentality throughout the company.

8. Develop an overall program with credibility.

Compensation can logically be divided into three components designed to accomplish three different goals:

1. Fixed-compensation salary.

2. Indirect-compensation benefits.

3. Variable-compensation incentives.

The success of the compensation program depends on its design and the attitude of individuals toward the compensation strategy. These two factors will determine the strategy's effectiveness. One of the failures of today's compensation programs is their focus on the company's perspective and failure to pay sufficient attention to the employee's perspective.

Salary is a fixed portion of the compensation picture for a given year, adjusted to reflect issues such as job responsibilities, seniority, and so on. Salary forms the basic building block of the compensation package with benefits and incentives added to form the total compensation strategy. Together, the components of fixed, indirect, and variable compensation relate total compensation to performance and describe the way the individual components of compensation are delivered as part of the company's compensation strategy.

Think of these components reinforcing one another, with salary forming the foundation, indirect compensation sitting alongside salary, and variable compensation resting on top of the other two as seen in Figure 8–6.

Of the three components of the compensation pyramid, incentives have the strongest opportunity to influence performance-related behavior. Let's use our example of Heavy

F I G U R E   8–6

Compensation Pyramid

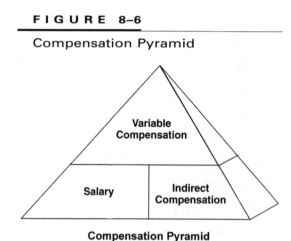

Compensation Pyramid

Capital Company to illustrate how incentives can be used to drive behavior.

There are many forms of incentive compensation. The combination of the way the incentives are earned (opportunity), their relationship to performance, their leverage, and the mechanism for delivering the payment can quickly become a complicated topic because of the number of combinations of opportunity, performance, leverage, and delivery designs. Let's begin by organizing the different considerations.

There are four factors in designing an incentive strategy. Each factor must consider individual design as well as the overall incentive strategy. Together, these factors help us design an incentive strategy with maximum effectiveness:

1. Opportunity.
2. Performance.
3. Leverage.
4. Delivery.

Opportunity Design

Opportunity design addresses the question of what will be earned and addresses four issues:

1. Participation.
2. Expected opportunity size.
3. Maximum payment.
4. Time horizon.

Participation addresses the issue of who participates in the opportunity. Where do you draw the line in determining who will and will not participate?

Expected opportunity size addresses the amount of the expected incentive payment. This is a difficult question, one that has no single answer because opportunity is a function of market pay conditions, meaningfulness of the opportunity to the individual, the economic perspective of the company, and the risk and opportunity offered in the other elements of compensation strategy.

Traditionally, incentive opportunities are calculated using market surveys. These methods are an important starting point in determining the meaningfulness of the incentive opportunity. Unfortunately, this information fails to take into account whether or not the incentive opportunity is meaningful to the individual. Wealth and attitude toward risk are prime determinants of the meaningfulness of an incentive payment, yet the data on these important issues is difficult to find. Figure 8–7 illustrates graphical representation of the relationship between the individual's wealth and risk attitudes, a determinant of incentive opportunities.

Figure 8–7 provides us with a starting point to think about the size of incentive opportunities beyond the traditional market-based survey data. Incentive pay may need to be artificially inflated to be successful due to the marginal impact of taxes on the net recovery to the employee or

Relationship of Wealth to Risk Tolerance

State of Wealth

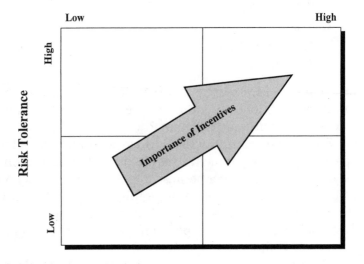

manager. Today, incentives are often used as pay-delivery mechanisms for tax purposes (for both corporate and individual incentives). Consequently, we see more pay being directed to the variable portion to take advantage of the variable-pay delivery mechanism and the tax rules that impact senior executive compensation.

Companies typically establish guidelines for market-pay comparisons and determine how they want to position themselves relative to their competition to the labor market. These guidelines are usually expressed as payment at different percentiles of the same job market. A company desiring to be very competitive might choose to pay as high as the 75th or 90th percentile of the market, while another company might choose to be more conservative and pay at the median 50th percentile. These market-pay comparisons represent interesting data but only reveal a small piece of the story. To fully assess the size of the expected opportunity, the market view needs to be assessed in light of how meaningful the award is.

A rule of thumb for thinking about the meaningfulness of an award is that the opportunity should be enough to get the individual focused on the desired results. Now, you may ask whether the company can motivate the individual to perform regardless of the incentive. Isn't there more to the job than the incentive? The answer is yes and no. Generally, people will perform as directed, but that is not what we are discussing here. We are talking about changing behavior. If we want to change a person's behavior, we must offer an incentive that makes the person take notice. People need to understand the company's strategy and how they can affect it to know what their performance means to the company.

There are a few tests we can apply when calculating the size of the incentive opportunity in order to make it meaningful enough to change behavior. Figure 8–8 shows a set of decision points and trade-offs to think through the size of the opportunity.

Maximum payments or caps are an issue because they influence the upper end of the opportunity. Some plans are capped; others are uncapped. There are both philosophical and practical reasons to cap or uncap incentive plans. Philosophically, you choose to uncap an incentive opportunity when you want to provide an unlimited upside opportunity. In essence, you are enlisting the individual as a partner to the company in the performance by sending the message, "As the company does better, so will you, with no limit on the upside."

Capped opportunities reflect a desire to reward the individual for outstanding performance up to some predefined limit. On the practical side, opportunities are capped for one of the following reasons:

FIGURE 8–8

Size of Expected Opportunity is Determined by Opportunity and Delivery

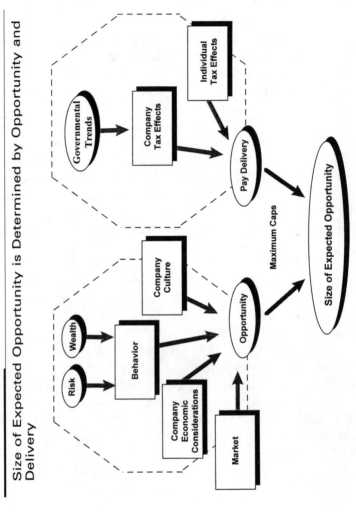

1. The link between the results of the company and the individual's performance is uncertain.
2. There is uncertainty in measuring the performance.
3. Company performance is volatile.
4. The payment might exceed the required incentive.

Caps are a way of protecting the company from over-paying for performance and balancing short- and long-term goals and performance. The decision to cap or uncap an opportunity has to be viewed in the context of an industry as well. Cyclical industries require different designs.

The time horizon for the incentives should match the company's business strategy as well as the needs of the individual. This can be difficult to accomplish because the timing interests of the various parties are often different. For example, the pharmaceutical industry experiences significant time to move from discovery of a chemical compound to FDA approval (10 to 15 years in some cases). Incentives cannot be that long or they lose meaning to individuals. As a result, it is tough to match the incentives (for example, three-year performance periods) with the time horizon of the business.

Time frame is another area where me-too incentive designs are the norm. Incentive time frames are justified based on common practice of other companies and not necessarily on the company's business strategy or its specific goals and objectives. Time frame in incentive design can support and reinforce the company's strategy instead of simply mimicking industry or competitor time frames. The right time frame for incentives is a function of the business strategy adjusted to reflect the needs of individuals—not the reverse.

Performance Design

Performance design addresses how the incentives are earned. Performance design includes deciding what measure(s) will be used, the weight of the measures, the degree of difficulty of goals and targets for the measures, and the choice of a targeted or sharing approach.

Selection of financial performance measures was explained in Chapter 7. In addition to the choice of financial performance measures, you may consider strategic measures. Strategic measures of performance augment the interpretation of the financial performance results by capturing elements of the strategy that do not show up in a single period's financial results. What is the right balance between single-period financial results and the strategic results that take longer to develop into financial results? The balance should be driven by each company's individual circumstances, recognizing that it will require more than a single period to accomplish the strategy. In general, the more short-term the strategy, the less the need for strategic measures. Conversely, the longer the time horizon, the greater the need for strategic measures to support, augment, and balance a single period's financial results.

Performance design should contemplate the nature of the performance by participant, as illustrated in Table 8–4.

When you select more than one performance measure, the relative importance of each measure must be assessed to determine the performance on which the incentive award will be based. For example, if you choose one measure of profitability and one of revenue growth, these two measures need to be weighted to reflect their relative performance in determining the incentive earned.

Degree of difficulty is an important consideration in the performance design because the degree of difficulty associated with the measure will affect the behavior of individuals. If you are using a measure of profitability such

T A B L E 8-4

Performance Profile

Nature of Performance	CEO	Sector EVP	SBU Head	Corporate Staff
Market	Shareholder value created relative to S&P 400	← Adjust for major market movements →		
Industry		Sector shareholder value created or financial measures relative to industry peers	← Adjust for major economic shocks →	
Business			Quantitative internal performance measures (Or sector relative SVC for dominant SBU's)	Individual objectives Quantitative and Non-financial

Source: SCA analysis.

239

as return on net assets, the minimum acceptable level of performance must be determined from an incentive performance perspective with an understanding of how that translates to the improvement required. The degree of difficulty must be benchmarked against what is possible, practical, and achievable. Too often, the hurdle for the performance measure is set too high or too low, and the goals for the incentive program fail to encourage the desired behavior as a result of the overly aggressive goals.

Targets for performance include absolute, relative, average, or cumulative targets. Many incentive plans have gone astray when setting the targets. The section on leverage design, later in this chapter, addresses the target-setting process and shows how targets are first attached to performance measures and then rolled into incentive design.

The performance design must also strike a balance between formulaic answers and the role of management discretion. Selecting the right targeted levels of performance is more difficult than you might imagine. Take the example of a diversified chemical company shown in Table 8–5. Actual earnings per share was within the range between the minimum threshold and maximum performance cap only 30 percent of the time between 1972 and 1992.

Risk Tolerance

One of the new and most interesting areas of performance design involves the use of risk. Financial risk is the probability of a monetary loss. People have different attitudes toward financial risk. In terms of incentives, monetary loss represents the lost opportunity an employee experiences from an incentive that does not pay out at the targeted payment level. Because of the differences in individual's attitudes toward risk and their tolerance for financial risk,

T A B L E   8–5

Case Example: Diversified Chemical Company
Historical EPS Relative to Incentive Range
(1972–1992)

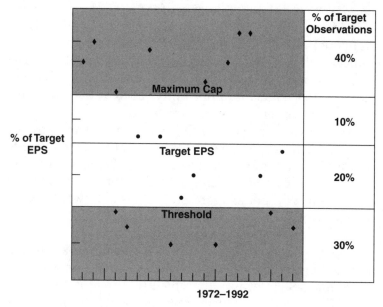

1972–1992

Source: SCA Analysis.

individual risk tolerance is an important element of incentive design.

Understanding the risk tolerance of individuals and matching them to the risk tolerance of others within the organization as well as the risk tolerance of the organization is essential for an effective compensation strategy.

Consider two individuals. The first individual is risk averse and would prefer a sure thing to the alternative of accepting much risk. The second individual is risk neutral and has the same preferences for a sure thing or accepting an opportunity for a greater opportunity involving risk if the expected values are the same for each alternative. In the second case, the risky alternative has a greater possibility for returns but involves some risk of receiving nothing.

When different people are offered the same incentive opportunity, they will value the opportunity differently because of their different tolerances for financial risk. The first individual, who is risk averse, will place a smaller value on the risky alternative than the second person, who is risk neutral, although the alternatives offer equivalent expected value. The amount of money is the same in both cases, but the value placed on the opportunity varies by the individual due to their different risk tolerance.

If the value placed on the opportunity varies by the way different people view risk, shouldn't we take this into account in planning an incentive strategy? The obvious answer is yes unless you prefer only one attitude toward risk in the company. Some aggressive CEOs only want people who share the same attitude toward risk in their organization.

This is not practical because risk tolerance is a function of two things: the individual's framework for risk and the individual's state of wealth, which has great influence on her or his level of financial risk tolerance. We learn risk tolerance as children. We grow up conditioned to think about the risks of the world (of which financial risks are a special subclass) differently, depending on our experiences and upbringing.

The second defining element of risk tolerance is the individual's state of financial wealth. All other things being equal, the wealthier the individual, the greater the individual's tolerance for risk. A millionaire is more comfortable losing $1,000 than is someone who has only $2,000 in the bank. These two factors of risk framework and state of wealth combine to determine the individual's financial risk tolerance. The more profoundly risk averse the individual's framework and the lower the state of financial wealth, the more risk averse the individual.

Understanding how people's risk tolerance affects the decisions they make is an important, yet poorly understood, area of compensation.

Screening people in the organization for risk frameworks would be difficult. Even if a CEO could screen the decision makers for their attitude toward risk, it would still not be possible to find enough individuals with the same state of wealth or sense of risk as the CEO. Is it any wonder that CEOs are constantly decrying the lack of risk taking in their companies? It is also not necessarily desirable to have the same attitudes toward risk everywhere in the organization. Do you really want a risk taker as the company lawyer? Do you want the same level of risk in operations as in new product development?

As discussed earlier in this chapter, the incentive programs in place today fail to recognize the potentially vast differences in risk tolerance of individual participants. This leads to a mismatch between the incentives and the strategies being pursued. The incentive plan designed to incent risk taking can unwittingly do the reverse and incent a risk-averse attitude, or the moderate risk plan can actually end up as a plan that encourages unsafe risks.

Is the organization tolerant of risk diversity? Is it going to have a one-size-fits-all incentive program? Is it willing to allow a range of incentive alternatives that includes different opportunities and contemplates differences in needs and risk tolerances while still focusing behavior on executing the strategy?

Let's return to our example of Heavy Capital Company, which is using return on equity (ROE) as the basis for their performance-oriented incentive design.

For Heavy Capital, it would make sense to add a measure of growth to the incentive design. Focusing solely on ROE has discouraged the capital investment required for the company to stay competitive. We know they are in a cyclical business by looking at the returns in Figure 8–3, so we have to maintain a focus on returns, but we can add a factor for growth and weight it equally with the ROE measure. The result will provide management with a better focus on profitable growth.

What relationship do you want between risk and reward? What is the relationship that best supports the strategy, and how will the incentive design put pay at risk and reward superior performance? The answers to these questions form the basis of what is known as leverage.

Leverage Design

Leverage is the risk/reward relationship of the incentives and the performance. The higher the leverage, the more incentives are paid per incremental improvement in performance. Take the example of General Motors, which chose to use return on net assets (RONA) as their measure of financial performance. GM wants to improve profitability, and using returns as the measure is appropriate to support that objective. Now if GM were to integrate RONA into the incentive system and tie 10 percent of a manager's total compensation to a range within 5 percent of RONA, they would undo any progress made by choosing RONA in the first place. This is because the amount of compensation at risk is too small and the spread in RONA returns are too large to drive behavioral change.

Setting the leverage involves determining the targeted incentive, the threshold level of performance required, and the maximum performance contemplated in the incentive plan. Constructing the leverage for a targeted approach in the incentive plan involves a five-step process:

1. Determine the target.
2. Determine the threshold.
3. Determine the maximum.

4. Define the interpolation between the target and the threshold.

5. Define the interpolation between the target and the maximum.

How much leverage is appropriate? How does the leverage reflect the risk reward of the plan? Should the opportunity be capped? How is the risk and reward of the performance aligned with the strategy? How are the components of the incentive aligned with each other? These questions can be answered by establishing the relationship between the performance measure(s) and the incentives to be paid. To properly answer these questions, we need to analyze the factors that are driving leverage from industry, strategy, and organizational perspectives. Table 8–6 lists some of the factors that influence leverage design.

Leverage can also be different at different levels of performance. For example, a plan might have a threshold of 90 percent of targeted performance. Once performance exceeds 90 percent of target, the incentives will be paid to participants at a ratio of 1 percent of incremental performance up to the targeted performance and then 2 percent above the targeted performance up to a maximum of 200 percent of target. Figure 8–9 illustrates this scenario.

T A B L E   8–6

Factors in Determining Leverage and Scope

Economic factor	■ Affordable level of incentive compensation
Performance factor	■ Minimum acceptable performance level for which awards are warranted
Historical factor	■ Performance and award levels relative to the past
Retention factor	■ Requirement to pay some award regardless of performance

246

FIGURE 8-9

Incentive Leverage

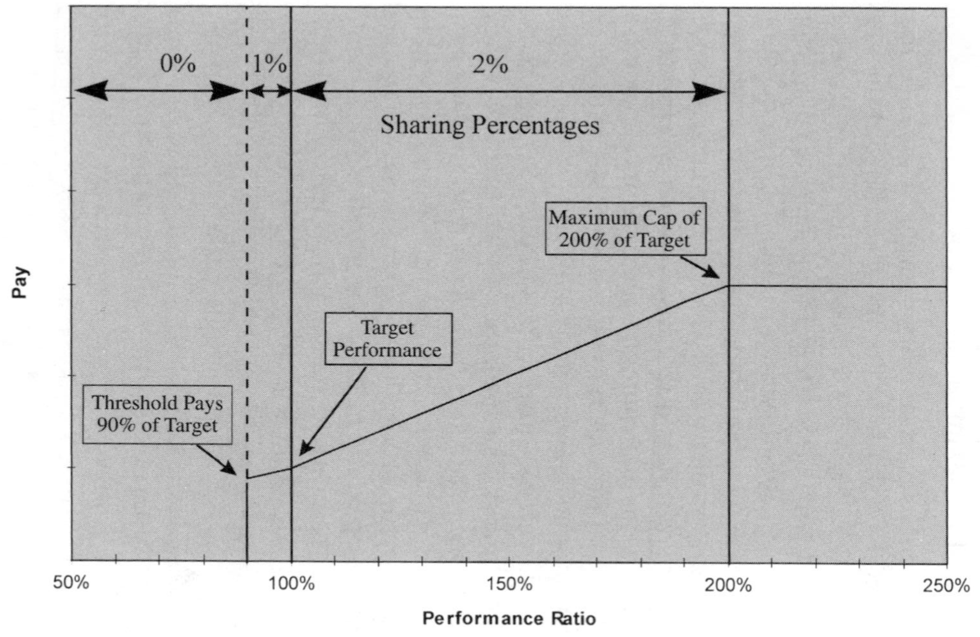

This is just one illustration of an infinite number of possible leverage relationships. We can change the relationship between the performance measure and the risk/reward ratio of the incentives by altering the leverage. Figure 8–10 illustrates that an increase and decrease in the risk/reward ratio can be achieved by altering the leverage. In this instance, we changed the sharing percentages, but the targets, thresholds, and maximums can also be changed. Removing the maximum is another way of altering the risk/reward ratio.

Leverage provides the opportunity to modify the incentive to both alter the risk/reward ratio and increase the focus on the performance measure at different leverage points, such as the threshold level and targeted performance.

A company's strategy is rarely static. It evolves over time and reflects changes in the underlying competitive situation. As company strategy evolves, so too should the compensation design. We can see this clearly in Figure 8–11, where the leverage was increased from 1988 to 1990 to reflect the changes in the company's strategy, resulting in an increased focus on performance.

Stock option programs that reward management for increases in the share price may have less risk to the executive than intended. They may actually be incenting the executives to do little if anything to alter the business strategy. In most stock option plans, the executive is getting a leveraged free ride on stock price appreciation with nothing at risk except foregone opportunities. These "first dollar" leveraged plans are in wide use today but create substantial problems because they price the value of the option grants with exercises prices at the current market value. The major variables in this type of valuation are the time value of money and rate of inflation in the economy. What risks, if any, is the individual being encouraged to take?

Sharing in the company's performance is an alternative

FIGURE 8-10

Altered Incentive Leverage

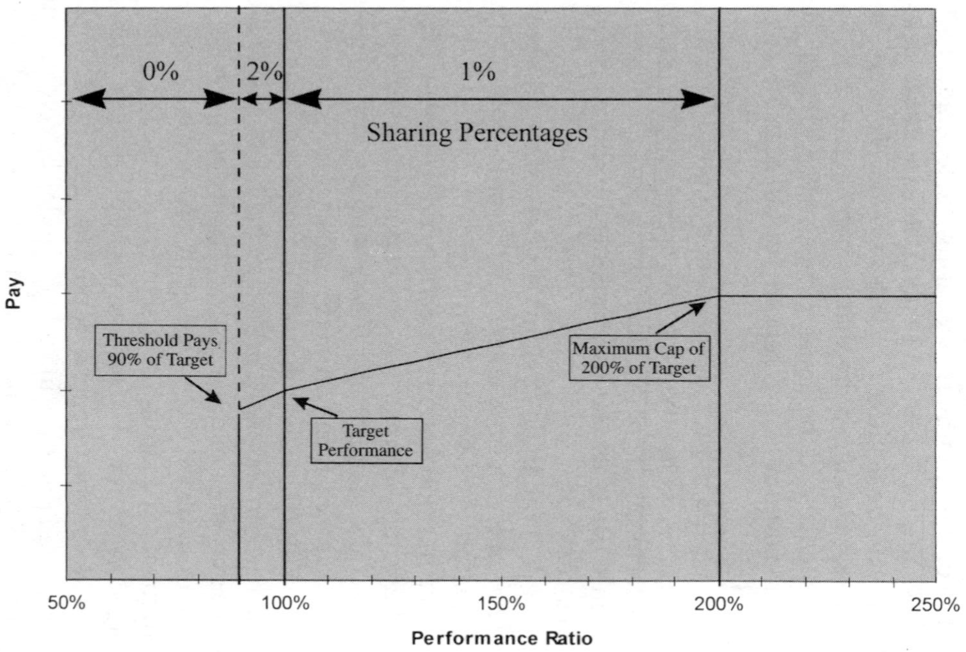

F I G U R E   8–11

Performance vs. Payout Various
Payout Opportunities

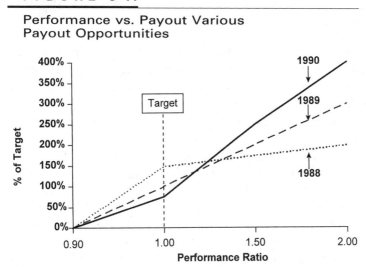

to setting targets. Sharing does not use targets but takes a different approach by making a share of the performance improvement or absolute performance available to the participant as an incentive. For example, if a company was earning $100 million, the company might agree to share 1 percent of the income above some minimum level. Conceptually, there is a large difference between targets and sharing. Targets presume the company management is able to set appropriate targets, while sharing makes no assumption about the ability of management to set targets and instead pays a share of the performance in the form of incentives regardless of the targeted amount. Targeting assumes a control-oriented, center-focused, hierarchical structure, while sharing assumes a collaborative, partnering approach. As companies move toward more self-directed work, sharing becomes a logical tool to support that strategy.

When sharing is used, the percentage to be shared needs to be determined. The amount of the share can be varied over the range of performance by setting inflection points. In addition to the sharing percentages, it may also be advisable to set thresholds and maximums. Figure 8–12 illustrates a simple sharing percentage over a range of performance where the sharing percentage is held constant and the opportunity is capped. Figure 8–13 illustrates a slightly more complicated variation that modifies the simple sharing percentage approach depicted in Figure 8–11 and introduces an inflection point where the percentage shared increases after a predetermined level of performance is achieved.

Performance and leverage design play a key role in incentive compensation where the intelligent use of risk can make an enormous difference in an organization. Recently, one company surveyed their senior management team and discovered that the risk attitude of the top two executives was substantially different than the risk attitude of the senior management team as a whole. The incentives that motivated the top two officers did not succeed with the rest of

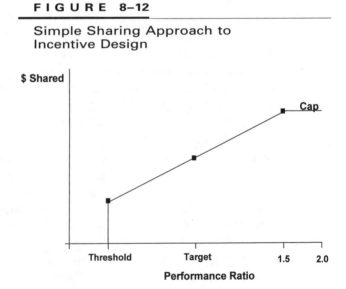

F I G U R E   8–12

Simple Sharing Approach to Incentive Design

Modified Sharing Approach to
Incentive Design

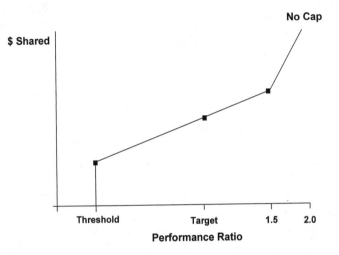

the team. The result of this dichotomy revealed itself in the
varied quality of decisions being made in the organization.
Managers were not willing to take the risks the top two
officers wanted. When the managers failed to take risks,
they were publicly criticized. These actions caused the other
members of the senior team to become even more risk
averse. The risk-averse climate led to a significant increase
in the amount of time senior management spent playing
politics trying to second guess the CEO.

Delivery Design

Delivery design includes the type of payment, use of stock
(real, phantom, and restricted), options (at-the-money, in-
the-money, and out-of-the-money), tax consequences to the
company and the individual, mix of payment, timing of the

payment, and restrictions affecting the delivery of incentives to participants.

Often, the design mechanisms are confused with the delivery strategy. This distinction is important because they have very different objectives. Design strategy should be optimized to support the company's strategy. Delivery mechanisms should reflect the strategy but be optimized to take advantage of the different methods available to minimize the after-tax cost to the company while maximizing the after-tax benefit to the participant. Placing pay at risk with the company's stock value is a design strategy. Choosing to use a 10-year nonqualified stock option is a delivery strategy. Choosing to make the option premium priced as a way to focus management on a minimum return is a strategic design issue. There are many mechanisms for delivering incentives that warrant a more complete treatment of the subject.[1]

The combination of opportunity design and delivery design is referred to as "mix." It affects behavior both by the way the incentive is earned and how it is paid. Mix establishes the individual's time orientation through a combination of long-term and short-term opportunities and the timing of their delivery. The right mix is one that achieves the appropriate balance between short- and long-term opportunities and reinforces behavior supportive of the business strategy.

Consider Heavy Capital Company, where the incentives are weighted 75 percent to the annual performance and 25 percent to the three-year performance. The effect of the long-term three-year plan is limited. Heavy Capital Company's managers placed very little emphasis on the long-term plan because it is too small and uncertain for them to control or impact. This example highlights a plan overly weighted to short-term incentives.

One way to think about the relationship between mix and time is to compare the risk of the delivery vehicle with the time horizon, as in Figure 8–14. The higher the risk, the longer the term.

F I G U R E   8–14

Relationship of Time Horizon and Risk

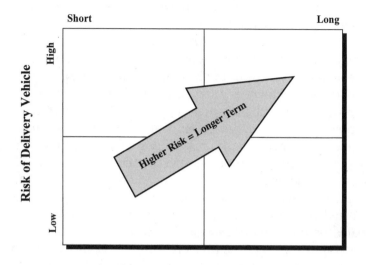

The mix between short- and long-term incentives is meant to address the time frame; however, it may not address the issue, depending on the company, its strategy, and the mix of incentives selected. Often, companies worry that the results might not be sustainable. Therefore, they don't want to pay out the results until they are more certain of the outcome. Time frame can also address the issue of consistency for the results generated. Measuring the results over a business cycle or capturing the performance relative to others in the industry can help to reinforce the desired behavior.

The mix of incentive delivery vehicles can influence the risk/reward relationship as well. For example, if you substitute stock options for restricted stock of equal expected value, the risk/reward relationship has changed to reflect the greater leverage inherent in the options. Mix of delivery vehicles becomes an important strategic tool for management to use to determine the best aligned leverage for the chosen strategy. Delivery should also address the tax considerations from the perspective of the company as well as the individual.

Restrictions can be time or performance based. They usually take the form of a time-based restriction that delays the actual payment of the incentive until a certain time has passed. Performance-based restrictions are tied to one or more performance measures and the achievement of certain targets. Time-based restrictions deal more with sustainability, while performance-based restrictions focus on achievability.

One topic that requires special mention in the delivery design is the problem of attracting and retaining key people in talent-based industries. Today, more executives are being treated like professional athletes or movie stars who are paid for their marquee value as well as their talent. Attracting these top executives requires substantial amounts of money, usually paid in the form of stock options designed to motivate the executive to create change. Examples of this trend include names such as George Fisher at Kodak, Louis Gerstner at IBM, and James Barksdale at Netscape. Table 8–7 compares CEO's pay with other prominent talented people.

Payment for talent is a special issue in delivery and is necessary in cases where the company wants to attract a rare person whose skills are in demand. In these cases, as with any other commodity in short supply, it will be necessary to "pay the bill" to attract these individuals. Properly designing pay packages for these individuals is even more critical than designing the typical incentive program because of the money involved and the lease opportunity costs. In trying to attract these name talents whose track records qualify them for star status, boards of directors, on behalf of the shareholders, gamble on the ability of this individual to accomplish the desired goals and create value.

TABLE 8-7

Notable Compensation
Packages

Athletes	
Mike Tyson	$75.0 million
Michael Jordan	$52.6 million
Shaquille O'Neal	$24.4 million
Entertainers	
Oprah Winfrey	$97.0 million
Michael Jackson	$45.0 million
Tom Cruise	$27.0 million
CEOs	
Louis Gerstner	$24.0 million
Jack Welch	$ 6.3 million
George Fisher	$ 4.7 million

In these cases, understanding the individual's risk tolerance and designing the incentive program to send the right signals is critical. Another issue involves the distinction between payments required to convince the individual to take the job and the payments required to motivate the individual on an ongoing basis.

Delivery is a complex issue because it involves elements of strategy and mechanisms for pure delivery. When the two are confused, the plan design reflects this confusion, resulting in a suboptimal design and less than satisfactory results.

Windfalls

Windfalls occur when the incentive pays the participant more than intended for the planned level of performance. Windfalls result from unanticipated performance improvement or incomplete incentive plan design. Unanticipated performance improvement is a function of either poor target setting or unanticipated events external to the company (for example, takeovers).

An example of poor incentive design might include a case where the performance measure was designed to incent improved returns but where management sells the business's strategic assets to achieve those returns. In this case, management has behaved in accordance with the incentive plan's design, even though it may not be in the best interests of the company. Taken to its extreme, a return measure can incent management to shrink the business to its highest performing unit, which may not be the right strategy. Aligning the incentive plan with the desired behavior is important if you want to reduce the probability of windfalls that result from counterproductive behavior.

Gaming

A variation on windfalls is gaming. Gaming is the practice of altering the results to best fit the measure so the incentive is maximized. An example of this might include overdelivering to customers at year-end to meet sales goals. These counterproductive games are played in many companies. RJR Nabisco is a notable example of a company that participated in gaming. In the book *Barbarians at the Gate,* there is a description of how RJR Nabisco gamed the earnings to make their sales goals by pushing up customer inventories at year-end. Higher sales resulted from moving the sales forward in time from the first quarter of the following year to the fourth quarter of the current year. Since there was no corresponding increase in demand for the product, the product sat on the wholesaler's or retailer's shelf until it was eventually sold to the end customer. This gaming led to a weaker first quarter each year as orders from wholesalers dropped due to the overshipment of inventory resulting from the fourth-quarter sales push.

Sandbagging

Another game is budget sandbagging. This game is played in many companies. The point of the game is to reduce the budget targets set for the performance measures to make them more achievable. This game is played out over the course of many months throughout the planning and budgeting cycle. The amount of time spent on this particular game is one of the great comic business tragedies. The politics and negotiations that surround budget targets is a sight to be seen. Imagine the productivity gains that could be realized from redeploying these negotiations into value-creating activities.

Decoupling the incentive target from the budget is an easy way to reduce sandbagging. As long as the incentives are tied to budget targets, there will be a very strong incentive to reduce the target. Hours, days, weeks, and sometimes even months are spent each year on sandbagging budget targets. What difference does it make if the person is good at negotiating a target—does it add value to the company? Why not take the same time and effort and make more products, sell more services, and improve customer relations?

Some gaming is innocent enough, driven by a simple desire to get the incremental order at the end of the year, but other types of gaming can lead to behavior that is not in the best interests of the company. The best defense against gaming is to spend sufficient time designing an incentive plan that works for the business and that is not just another "me-too" plan.

INNOVATIVE PERFORMANCE-
BASED PROGRAMS

In recent years, a series of innovative performance-based incentive plans have been designed. The design features include many of the issues of opportunity, performance, leverage, and delivery we have discussed. Designs that warrant special mention include premium-priced options, leveraged equity, and banking. These programs are having a profound positive influence on results. They raise the focus on value creation and support strategy execution.

Premium-Priced Options

Premium-priced options are options granted out-of-the-money. The concept behind these options is to provide the investor with a return on their investment in front of the management and to then share a greater percentage of the value above the target return with the management team. Commerce Clearing House is one company that has used this design successfully.

Leveraged Equity

Another innovative program is performance-based leveraged equity. In this case, senior managers borrow money from the company to buy the company's stock in the open market. The design may also include reducing capital at risk over time if certain performance criteria are met. These programs have received very positive reviews from investors and managers; in fact, Monsanto's stock increased 5 percent on the day the performance-based leverage equity plan was announced.

Banking

Banking is a term coming into wider use today. The concept behind banking is simple. The bank is a mechanism to make sure the performance delivered by management is sustainable before paying the incentive. Typically, an account (bank) is set up and one-third the amount of the incentive earned in the year is paid out to the individual in the current year. Two-thirds is retained in the bank and paid out in equal installments over the coming two years, providing the performance on which the original award was made is maintained. There are many variations on the banking idea that include restrictions for performance and time. Many companies are using banking and finding it helpful as a tool for incentive plan design. These are only three of the innovative designs in use today. In each case, the design supports the company's strategy and is focused on delivering value to the shareholders.

CONCLUSION

Incentives are a powerful tool to influence behavior. When properly constructed, they represent a strategic tool that helps drive performance. Far too often, incentives are relegated to the back room of decision making because line managers do not really understand how to use them effectively. When you include incentives in your value-management program, they can help you achieve the full potential of your company's strategy to create value. The next chapter will describe how to implement value-based management.

Implementing Value-Based Management

Value management can only be successful in a company if the decision makers understand what it is and how they can affect value creation through their decisions. To achieve success in value management, the company needs to integrate value-based decision making throughout the organization. Integrating value-based decision making into a company requires answering three questions:

1. What are value management and value-based decision making?
2. Why are we implementing value management?
3. How can individuals affect value creation?

The difference between success and failure of value-based decision making is determined by the quality of a company's implementation. Successful implementation is critical for the principles and practices of value-based decision making to take root and grow.

KEY IMPLEMENTATION SUCCESS FACTORS

Successful implementation requires a clear and articulate case to be made supporting the use of value-based decision

making throughout the organization. This clarity of purpose is accomplished by thoughtfully translating the principles, concepts, and practices of value-based decision
making into the language of the business. Since value is
an abstract concept that few people intuitively understand,
they may not fully comprehend their individual impact
on value creation for the company. The overriding goal
is to make everyone in the company understand how
they can create value through their individual actions
and decisions. Accomplishing this goal means translating
the value concepts from abstract ideas into the reality of
day-to-day business decisions about how and where a
company's resources are allocated. This translation must
include an intuitive understanding of why value management is important for the company, what value is, and
how to affect it.

Successful implementation of value-based management requires managing several critical variables. The exact
formula will vary from company to company and industry
to industry, but the basic building blocks for implementation remain the same:

- Senior management leadership and commitment.
- Fit with management processes.
- Education and training.
- Communication.
- Time horizon and task sequencing.
- Champions (content and process).

The next few sections will discuss each of these building
blocks, highlighting how use of the building blocks can
improve the chances for a successful implementation.
Implementation occurs through repeatedly emphasizing
value concepts in decision making, thereby altering the key
management processes including: planning, budgeting,
management reporting, and incentive compensation.

SENIOR MANAGEMENT LEADERSHIP
AND COMMITMENT

Senior management needs to address a combination of issues to ensure the successful implementation of value-based decision making. First, senior management must be aware of the program and sponsor it. Sponsorship means that senior managers acknowledge the importance of the program among the company's other priorities. Ideally, senior management sponsorship will not be limited to a single executive but will extend to a significant portion of the senior management team.

Senior management needs to demonstrate its commitment by showing interest in the value program. Interest can take many forms, whether it is asking about the implementation progress, querying the details of the underlying financial calculations supporting the performance measures, or discussing how management decision making is changing as a result of the implementation. Senior management must demonstrate interest in public forums where other managers in the company can see their commitment. The goal is to engage senior management's interest and support but to limit their involvement to prevent undue tinkering with every detail of the value program.

Senior management is and will remain the guardian of the company's resources. As such, they will be required to make sufficient resources available for the value program to be successful. Typically, the expense in dollars is not significant. However, the investment of managerial time for both managers and employees can be a required resource that is often not well understood or anticipated. Time is a real cost today because in most organizations there is a finite amount of available management time, and there are usually conflicting priorities screaming for attention. The business has to be run, costs have to be cut, earnings goals must be met, and the CEO has a new idea for the business that he wants explored. Sounds familiar, doesn't it?

Yet through this haze of conflicting priorities, multiple tasks, and overcommitment, senior management needs to support the value program by allocating the necessary resources in the form of people's time and energy. These resources are both overt and subtle commitments. An overt commitment of resources involves a management team to lead the implementation effort and weave the concepts into the planning, budgeting, incentives, and management reporting. As for more subtle resources, a few well-chosen words by senior managers can have an enormous influence on how tasks get prioritized in the organization. It is this prioritization that will facilitate the implementation because it emphasizes and reinforces the importance of the task. The message must be consistently delivered: "Yes, there are goals for this quarter's earnings that have to be met, but the value program is crucial to the long-term competitive position of the company, and therefore it requires equal attention."

Senior management should not only talk the talk, they should walk the walk. This means that senior management must not only provide verbal support for the value program but must also be perceived as taking action, thereby demonstrating a commitment to the value program. The difference is important because a number of value implementations have failed from a lack of perceived senior management commitment.

One instance where senior management fell short occurred in a $5 billion media company. The company was committed to a value program and was making progress integrating the value program into the way decisions were made. One morning, the CEO (who fully supported the initiative) was at a breakfast for mid-level managers and offhandedly referred to the value program as, "that program I can't remember the name of." The effect was instantaneous. Mid-level managers in attendance at the breakfast informed their peers that the CEO was not really committed to value. As these words quickly spread through the company, the unintended effect of the offhanded comment became apparent, setting back the value programs' implementation almost a year. It took almost a full year to earn back the trust and respect of some of the key managers and convince them that this was an important program that had the CEO's blessing.

There are many opportunities for senior managers to communicate the importance and urgency of the value program within the company. The CEO should use every budget, monthly status update, or planning review meeting to ask questions supporting the case for value-based decisions. For example, in one company, the CEO used value as the language of the quarterly budgeting discussions. The message to the operating management was clear: "Value is important to me; you'd better know this!"

FIT WITH MANAGEMENT PROCESSES

Value-based decision making must be required across the four key management processes. The decision-making environment should reinforce value-based decisions from all directions, and the management processes (planning, budgeting, incentives, and reporting) ideally should reinforce the same messages. Imagine being on the receiving end of communications concerning the various corporate processes and finding that each of them has different priorities, time horizons, and champions and that the signals from the different sources are at times inconsistent. Planning is telling you to invest while your compensation incentives are telling you to cut costs to make the earnings numbers. If you are like most people, you are likely to be confused by the conflicting messages.

Establishing clear messages and consistent signals in all management processes is important for the success of a value program and for the execution of the company's

strategy. Aligning the key management processes represents an important opportunity for many companies where
garbled messages and inconsistent signals have become a
barrier to good decision making.

EDUCATION AND TRAINING

In addition to the time commitment and priority setting,
senior management will also need to commit resources to
developing a combination of training and education programs for the company. To be most effective, these training
and education programs should be customized to the company's business issues. Standard education on value concepts is a necessary step, but don't count on standard education to develop commitment inside the company. An
education and training program that addresses the specific
business issues the company is facing will be far more meaningful. This helps make the value program a meaningful
decision-making tool.

Change of any kind requires education, and value management is no exception. Successful value-management implementation relies on significant education for many different groups in the company.

There are two goals for an education and training
program:

1. Build awareness of the value concepts and why
   they are important.
2. Integrate the concepts into the day-to-day
   decisions management makes.

Only by integrating the concepts into daily decision making
can the value-management program achieve its full potential. Companies have tried a variety of approaches to achieve
these two goals, with varying levels of success.

The few companies that have gone the complex route
and tried to make their managerial staff into financial man-

agers have failed because the task is too great and the willingness of the operating manager to become a financial manager is low. Conversely, the companies that have tried to use a simple, one-size-fits-all approach and train everyone using generic material have failed because the material is either not meaningful enough to the business or it is not robust enough to help in real decision making.

If the education and training is to be effective, it needs to be company-specific and contain material that illustrates how value concepts can and should be used to improve decision making. To be successful, education should also be:

- For line and staff managers.
- Baseline and technical.
- Up-front and ongoing.
- Mandatory.
- Based on the company's business.

Staff and line management need to be introduced to the concepts of value, and the concepts should be related to their decisions. Education is desirable on many levels to improve the understanding of the value concepts and reduce the anxiety associated with change. Each group of staff and line managers needs both general and specific education. The technical training in value computations should be reserved for the keepers of the numbers, while the broad underlying concepts should be introduced to all. Technical education on value is best suited for the finance and planning staffs who are the custodians of managerial reporting systems. The majority of managers should be introduced to the concepts of value. The concepts need to be illustrated with examples of real-life decisions.

Education should be a two-way exercise used to both enhance understanding and to uncover any specific business issues that might impede or slow adoption of the value program. If education is used wisely, it can go a long way to dispelling concerns over the unknown and reducing the resistance to change within the organization.

The purpose of education is to support implementation of the value program. If this objective is going to be met, education cannot be a one-shot activity that is removed from the business. Instead, education has to be up-front and ongoing and related closely to the business issues facing the company. A single course in training will not change behavior. Altering the way decisions are made requires repetition over time and positive reinforcement. To achieve success with education, plan on a multi-year commitment. Otherwise, you are wasting money because education that is not relevant, repeated, and reinforced has a very short lifespan and little impact, if any. This conclusion leads to the next point: Education should be mandatory for everyone, including senior management. Education is expensive, and customized education costs even more. Without a tangible link to the company's business and the issues management is facing in the real world, education will prove to be an expensive exercise that is unlikely to yield any meaningful results.

The challenge with an education program is to locate a method and an educational level where the material is simple enough to be readily understood and absorbed while specific enough to be a meaningful tool for improved decision making. Rarely do off-the-shelf training programs satisfy the needs of companies. Companies that have tried the one-size-fits-all approach find themselves doing training and education for a second time on a customized basis.

An example of successful education is a railroad company that chose return on total capital as a measure of performance. The company invested the time and resources to illustrate for each manager in the company how they could influence value creation. The education seminars were held regularly over three months. The focus of the seminars was on helping each manager identify the ways they could affect the measure in the daily decisions they faced.

COMMUNICATION

Communication is essential for people to understand value creation and discover how the decisions they make influence the amount of value created. Internal communication is both an opportunity to speed implementation and a tool to improve results during implementation. Communication explains what value-based decision making is and is not. You can think of communication as the ongoing process of education, where the education programs themselves are discrete events.

To be successful, a communication program has to have the four Rs:

- Repetition.
- Reinforcement.
- Reception.
- Redundancy.

One-shot messages won't do it. A successful communication program requires the message to be *repeatedly* delivered. Just as in advertising, you need repetition to build awareness. The same is true for the value program. Say it once, say it twice, then say it again.

Periodic *reinforcement* is essential for successful communication. Ideally, periodic reinforcement becomes part of the management process, which accomplishes two things. First, managers receive the periodic reinforcement necessary to continue building the understanding necessary to use value concepts in their daily decision-making process. At the same time, the management processes are reinforcing the focus on value.

One of the success factors required for effective communication is how well the value concept is taught to and

received by the manager. Without sufficient training, the
manager will not be able to use the concept for the decisions
he or she must make. Only when the application of value
concepts is clearly defined, reinforced, and thoroughly reviewed, can the manager make intelligent decisions. This
is accomplished by translating the language of value into
the language of operations. For example, the language of
value uses the term capital efficiency. The more efficient
the capital, the greater the value. At Dell Computer, the
management team has taken the concept to heart and reduced the time to collect cash from their customers from
an industry average of 30 days to 1 day. In this case, the
language of operations is cash-conversion cycle time.

Redundancy means putting the concepts of value into
as many of the company's activities as possible. Redundancy will enhance the communication effort by increasing
the number of times the manager is exposed to value concepts and their application.

When it comes to implementation, it is hard to over-
communicate the purpose, intent, and strategies for value-
based decision making. The greater the internal communication, the faster the implementation, and constructing a good
communication program can be an indispensable tool for
better implementation. Internal communication should start
with each of the key management processes and then branch
out into the operating decision making. Internal communication in planning involves stating goals clearly and providing direction. As business plans are completed, the iterative
communication involved in the planning process should
emphasize the value consequences of the business plan.

When a company expresses its goals and strategies in
terms of value, investors and analysts do stand up and take
notice. Look at the sample of companies that adapted value
management in Figure 9–1 and you can see how communication of superior value creation to the investment commu-
nity has led to higher stock prices. When management

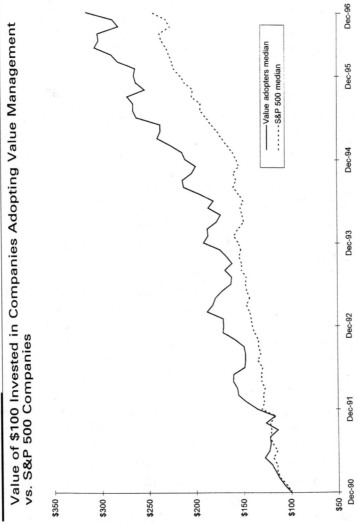

FIGURE 9-1

Value of $100 Invested in Companies Adopting Value Management vs. S&P 500 Companies

——— Value adopters median

······ S&P 500 median

speaks in terms of value, they are speaking the language of investors and analysts. Of course, just talking about value is not good enough; analysts and investors can quickly see through management that uses *value* as their most recent buzzword.

TIME HORIZON AND TASK SEQUENCING

Often, senior management adopts the value religion but misses the point of the sermon. Like most new religious converts, they develop a special zeal that waits for no one. Too often, senior managers command the corporate staff to go out and get some of that "EVA stuff" as some sort of magic elixir for what ails the company. If you are going to change the way decisions are made in the organization, plan on setting expectations for a multiyear process. Real problems are not solved with a magic potion but over time and with a focus on improvement.

Expectations can pose a difficult problem. If the company is sold on the idea that a value program will provide instant results, they will be disappointed. You can talk to anyone from Jack Welch (CEO of GE) to Roberto Goizueta (CEO of Coca-Cola), and they will tell you the true realization of value comes from improved decision making. If you take the time early in the value program to set senior management expectations and keep them updated regularly with progress and war stories, you will improve the chances for successful implementation.

Change takes time. The transformation of a company is a multifaceted, multiperiod, and multidisciplined process. Allow the improved decision-making time to take root at the operating levels of the company, while fertilizing the program with success stories from inside or outside the company. Think of the required time in the context of a change process. The change process in large organizations takes longer than in small organizations. One multinational consumer goods company has been involved in the change process for two years and is likely to be in it for another two. In a smaller high-technology company, the total time horizon collapses to two years. The implementation time horizon can vary from a period as short as one year to as long as four or more years because implementation of a value program alters the way the company makes decisions. The actual time horizon for implementation depends on the type of company, the organizational structure, resistance to change, and availability of information.

Excellent implementation takes time, whether you are implementing value or a new distribution system at Wal-Mart. The time horizon is an important consideration. Be realistic in the time horizon you select for implementation. Change is a difficult process, and large-scale organizational change that affects decision making is complex. Setting unrealistic time expectations can be the death knell of an implementation program because when expectations are not met, managers come to view the program as a failure or as ineffective, which leads to a reprioritization of the implementation program. Think carefully about time horizon and task sequencing and be realistic in setting time frames and expectations. Figure 9–2 shows the time frames involved for three different types of companies that implemented value-based management.

The correct sequencing of implementation is as important as the time horizon in setting expectations. In some companies, it makes sense to lead by changing the incentive system, while in others, leading by changing the incentive system will render the value program dead on arrival. What is at work here is the corporate culture.

Some company cultures are far more centralized than others. In these cases, the value program can be led from the center of the company through bold moves such as changing the compensation program.

Other companies are more consensus driven. In these

FIGURE 9-2(a)

An Example of a Value-Based Management-Implementation Process

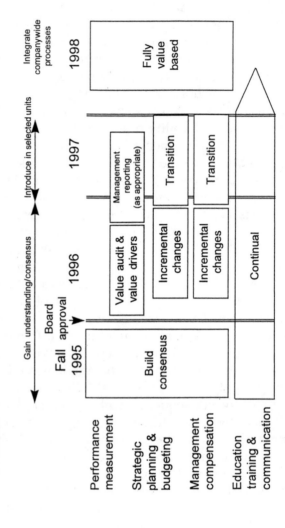

FIGURE 9-2(b)

An Example of a Value-Based Management-Implementation Process

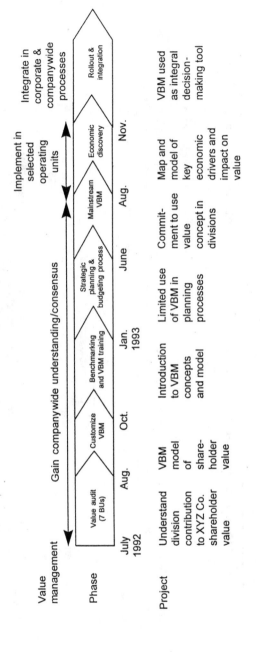

Value management			Gain companywide understanding/consensus		Implement in selected operating units		Integrate in corporate & companywide processes
Phase	Value audit (7 BUs)	Customize VBM	Benchmarking and VBM training	Strategic planning & budgeting process	Mainstream VBM	Economic discovery	Rollout & integration
	July 1992	Aug.	Oct.	Jan. 1993	June	Aug.	Nov.	
Project	Understand division contribution to XYZ Co. shareholder value	VBM model of shareholder value	Introduction to VBM concepts and model	Limited use of VBM in planning processes	Commitment to use value concept in divisions	Map and model of key economic drivers and impact on value	VBM used as integral decision-making tool

275

FIGURE 9-2(c)

An Example of a Value-Based Management-Implementation Process

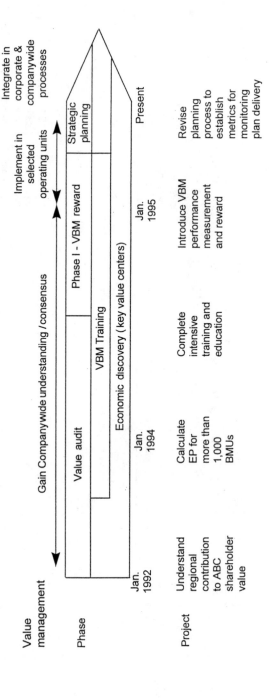

Value management	Gain Companywide understanding / consensus		Implement in selected operating units	Integrate in corporate & companywide processes
Phase	Value audit	Phase I - VBM reward	Strategic planning	
		VBM Training		
		Economic discovery (key value centers)		
	Jan. 1992	Jan. 1994	Jan. 1995	Present
Project	Understand regional contribution to ABC shareholder value	Calculate EP for more than 1,000 BMUs	Complete intensive training and education	Introduce VBM performance measurement and reward	Revise planning process to establish metrics for monitoring plan delivery

companies, a premature change to the compensation system will reduce the chances of success for the value program. In consensus-driven culture, the sequencing of implementation steps should begin with education and training and follow a path of ever-increasing communication. In consensus-based companies, it makes sense to include the value program in planning, budgeting, and other management processes before installing it in compensation. Often, these companies prefer to run the value program in parallel with the existing management processes for a year before going "live" with the value program as a full decision-making tool. This gives people in the company the chance to become familiar with the concepts of value and how the concepts pertain to their jobs and to them personally before being forced to make decisions based on value. The risk in consensus companies is that the implementation will get bogged down and die a slow death from never being fully ratified as a primary and legitimate decision-making tool. For this reason and others, it makes sense to have a value champion in the company.

CHAMPIONS (CONTENT AND PROCESS)

Champions are respected managers in the company who carry the torch for the implementation program. There are two different types of champions: content champions and process champions. Each is integral to the success of the implementation process but provides very different skills to the successful value program.

The content champion focuses on making sure the measure accurately captures the underlying business economics. This individual is the "go-to" person for all questions about value and becomes the keeper of the rule book for the measures. This champion need not be the most senior manager in the company but should be respected for her or his ability to understand the business issues and to discuss decisions and business issues where the performance measures might affect behavior.

The role of the content champion is to understand the company's business issues and their implications on decision making, performance measurement, and incentive design. The content champion must be versed in the nuances of performance measurement calculations and incentive design and be able to answer most questions from staff and line managers. The content champion becomes the de facto lead trainer in the organization. Although he or she does not train everyone on the technical details, the content champion is available to answer questions that stump the typical trainer. The content champion becomes a resource for the company and an internal arbiter regarding the application of value concepts. Typically, this content champion is on the CFO's staff.

The second type of champion is the process champion. In smaller companies, this individual is the same as the content champion, but in large companies the process champion is usually a different person. The role of the process champion is to manage the implementation process. The process requires just as much if not more attention than the content of implementation. The process champion should focus on organizational buy-in and monitor the level of commitment to value in the organization. The process champion knows how to get the organization to change, where the key points of leverage are, and how to influence other decision makers in the company. The process champion works the company network, understands the company culture, and unearths possible objections to the value program so they can be addressed before they mushroom into major controversies. Typically, the process champion is a person familiar with the company's questions, is respected by managers, and is thought of as a fair and unbiased facilitator. In smaller companies, the process and content champions may be the same people.

SUMMARY

The combination of senior management commitment, integration of value into the management processes, education of staff and line managers, communication, appropriate time horizons, and champions form the building blocks for successful implementation. The building blocks put in place the capabilities the company will use to attain the objectives of the value-based program. When the building blocks for successful implementation are integrated with and tied to the corporate processes, the decision makers in the company are more likely to focus on managing for value. The results are definitely worth the effort of implementation.

CHAPTER 10

Why Value
Management Fails

Improving decision making and increasing management focus are good ideas. If high value-creating companies have used value-based decision making and seen the advantages for so long, why aren't all companies using it? The answer is twofold. First, there are those that have not tried managing for value seriously. They have their reasons, but often these reasons depend on their belief in one of two myths that surround the adoption of value management. The second reason companies may not use value management is their failure to implement value-based decision making. The most notable example of a company that tried value-based management and failed is Quaker Oats. We'll discuss this case in some detail later. First, let's look at the myths that prevent companies from trying value management.

WHY NOT TRY VALUE MANAGEMENT?

Two prevalent myths exist among the companies that have not adopted value management. The first is a belief that the business they are running is different from other businesses.

They believe that the business needs to be managed through their knowledge and expertise and that value management would get in the way of their judgment. The second myth is an abiding faith in the power of earnings per share and that all management has to do is take care of earnings, and the value creation will take care of itself. Let's examine these myths in more detail.

Myth 1: Our Business is Different; Value Management Will Not Work Here

This myth is usually perpetuated by managers who prefer the "seat-of-the-pants" management style. Although not always spoken, the thoughts underlying this type of management are best expressed as, "I know how to manage this business. The success of this business depends on my unique knowledge of the business. No one knows as much as I do."

This attitude is particularly prevalent in talent-intensive businesses such as high technology, entertainment, and parts of the financial services industry. In these industries, where talent is one of the key value drivers, the belief is that management tools such as value management will only get in the way of the talent that is creating value. Actually, the reverse is true. These industries have the greatest need for a structured approach to managing for value. In talent-intensive industries where the talent is the largest contributor to the value created for the owners, the talent is likely to extract from the owners large pieces of the value created for themselves.

You see this phenomena in the star investment bankers on Wall Street who receive very large annual compensation for their services. If we look at the total value created in the investment banks and divide up the value between the talent and the owners, we find that a large proportion of the value created goes to the talent and that a much smaller percentage goes to the owners. The same relationship holds true in the entertainment industry, where the talent extracts huge percentages of the value created. We saw data on this in Chapter 8.

Another example of this "I know best" attitude can be found in European companies. These companies tell you that the principles of value management are fine but they won't work in European companies because of the unique relationships between the management, owners, and employees. It is true that a large percentage of European companies are owned by either banks or by related companies through cross-holdings. This ownership structure provides a level of insulation from the realities of the marketplace and the investors' demands for consistent returns. But the walls that insulate management are coming down in Europe, and the movement to decentralize ownership and break up industrial cross-holdings is underway. European managers ignore these trends at their own peril because the insulation will not last forever.

There may be cases where the management is so uniquely talented that no one else can do the job, but usually this attitude is a smoke screen for an unwillingness to adopt a systematic approach to planning. The best proof that value management works in most industries is that, although it is not necessarily called by the same name, managing for value is practiced in almost every industry.

Myth 2: All We Need to Do Is Manage Earnings

Ask Apple Computer, Browning Ferris, or Waste Management if earnings are all that matters, and they will tell you there is more to managing for value than just growing earnings. Each of these companies focused on their earnings growth rates under the assumption that if you manage earnings, the value will take care of itself. However, investors were smart. They understood that although those companies were growing and delivering earnings growth, the returns on the new growth were nowhere near the returns on the existing business. Figure 10–1 illustrates the uneven, but positive earnings per share and the drop in returns for Waste Management from 1990 through 1995. Earnings tell an important piece of the story but only a piece. In each case, when returns fell, the result was a major hiccup for the company. There is more to managing a company and delivering value to shareholders than just growing earnings.

IMPLEMENTATION TRAPS

Let's turn our attention to the companies that have tried value management and failed. These are interesting examples because we can learn from their experiences what traps to avoid.

If we look at the unsuccessful implementations of value management that have failed in the last 10 years, we find they break down neatly into five traps. If you are not aware of these traps, you may stumble into them and pay the consequences.

Trap 1 : Flying by the Seat of the Pants

This trap is a painful one. Those companies that fell into this trap lacked a true commitment to value-based decision making. Usually, the lack of commitment is due to a lack of senior management commitment. This was the story underlying the well-known failure of value-based management principles at Quaker Oats.

Quaker Oats adopted value management in the late 1980s. Quaker widely claimed to be using the principles of value management extensively in their planning, budgeting, and incentive compensation. William Smithburg, Chairman of Quaker, talked about the commitment to economic value

FIGURE 10–1

Earnings Per Share vs. Return on Net Assets Waste Management

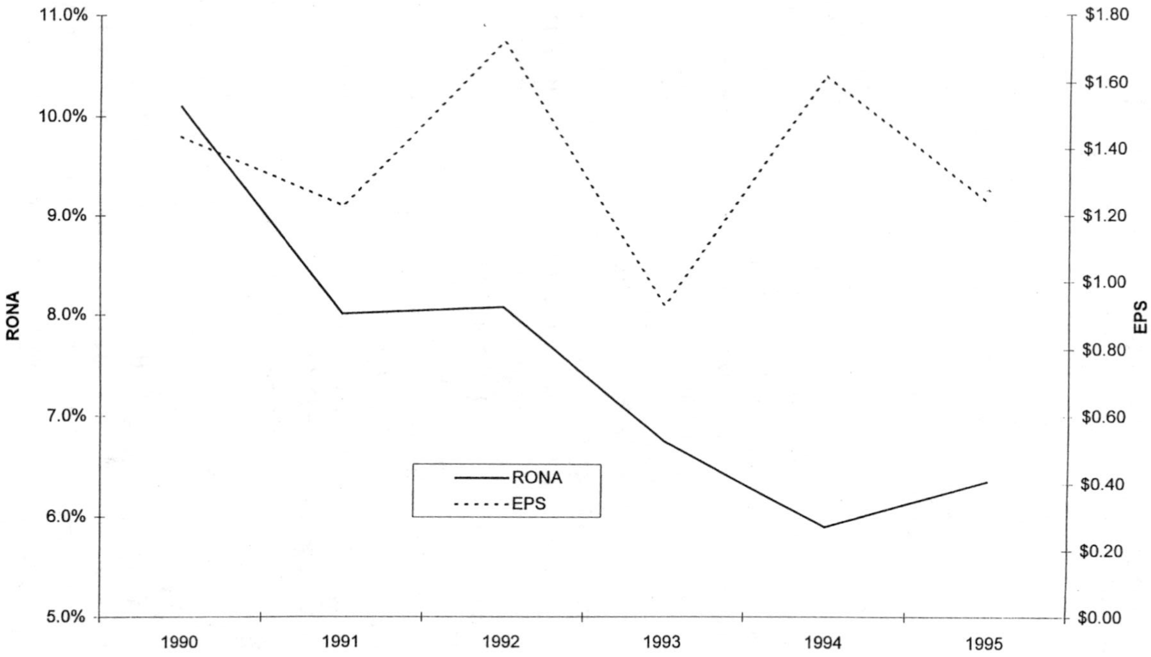

285

added and value management and in an April 1993 article
in *Enterprise Magazine* observed:

> What's the best way to deliver enduring shareholder re-
> turns? Focus on a concept called Economic Value Creation.
> Well, I certainly sleep better at night knowing our divisions
> are clearly focused on the things that will contribute to
> shareholder value.

Here is a company that from all outward signs was very
committed to managing the company for value. But Quaker
stock performance over this period was lackluster to disap-
pointing. The truth is that value management was a failure
at Quaker because senior management was never truly committed to the program.

Figure 10–2 compares the value Quaker created for
its shareholders relative to their peer group of food and
beverage companies from 1990 through 1996. Quaker is at
or close to the bottom in return to shareholders. If Quaker
is using value management, why is their performance so
poor? One clue to help answer the question lies in their
1994 acquisition of Snapple. The Snapple acquisition was a
big deal for Quaker. Snapple's stated book value of equity
was $162 million. Yet, Quaker paid $1.7 billion for the acquisition, representing a 10.5 multiple over book value. We
can determine the assumptions required to pay for this
premium over book value by using a simple cash flow multiple.

At the time of the acquisition, the price paid was the
highest price per case of soft drink in the consumer beverage
industry. Quaker paid that price believing they could absorb
the brand into their distribution system. Unfortunately, they
never discovered in their due diligence that many of the
Snapple distributors had tight contracts for geographic
areas that could not be broken; therefore, it was not possible
to easily mesh the Snapple distribution with the existing
Quaker distribution. At the same time, the competition in

FIGURE 10-2

Value of $100 Invested Quaker Oats vs. Peer Group Median

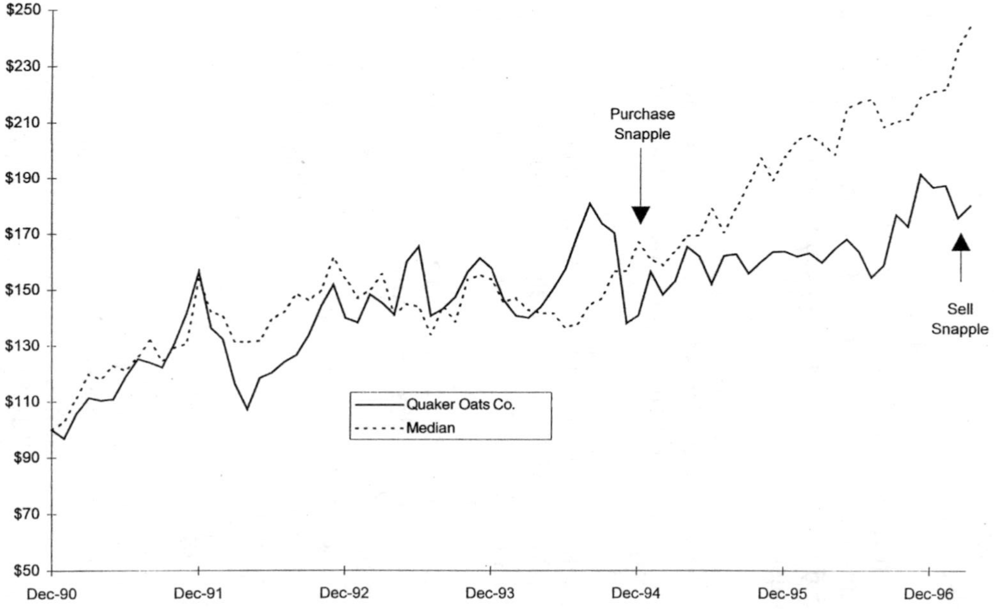

the specialty high-end soft drink market exploded with the introductions of new products by Lipton and aggressive marketing pushes by Arizona Iced Teas and Nantucket Nectars.

Quaker's sales had been growing at a rate of 4.5 percent from 1992 to 1995, which was well below their peers, whose sales were growing at 8.7 percent. Snapple was discussed in the company's 1995 annual report as a vital strategic acquisition:

> We expect to obtain this growth by bringing high-quality, value-added brands to consumers, and by delivering reliable service and greater profit opportunities to our customers. It is also why we acquired Snapple beverages.

Quaker believed that Snapple, when combined with Quaker's existing Gatorade business, would drive substantial growth for the company in the future. If the size and nature of this acquisition was so meaningful to Quaker, you would assume they had conducted an extensive value analysis regarding the acquisition and the price they were paying. Unfortunately, that was not the case. So, if Quaker did not use value management in calculating the Snapple acquisition, which was one of the most important strategic moves for the company in a decade, why should they use it in other decisions? If the value-based decision making cannot be trusted for the really important decisions, the implementation is bound to derail.

Smithburg could have used the Snapple acquisition as an important endorsement of value-based decision making. Instead, the company undermined their value-management efforts with a "fly-by-the-seat-of-the-pants" approach to the acquisition. One can only assume that the reason value was ignored or not used as a measure resulted from an unfavorable signal obtained from the value measure, which suggested the price they were paying was too high for the value they were receiving. If that is the case, then the message indicated that the company was not really using value to drive its big decisions. Flying by the seat of the pants doesn't always get you where you want to go. Quaker has had to learn that lesson the hard way. The lesson culminated in a loss of $1.2 billion, almost 70 percent of the purchase price, when Quaker agreed to sell Snapple in 1997.

Trap 2: Unrealistic Expectations

Unrealistic expectations can easily derail the value-management program. Often, senior management wants a quick fix to the problems they are confronting. Senior management may identify value as one of the programs that holds promise for addressing the ills that beset the company. After a quick review, senior management gives the go-ahead to a value-management program with the understanding that time is of the essence and that the program has to be rolled out to the company quickly to address the ills the company is trying to rectify. In these cases, the decision is usually to blast the value-management program into place as quickly as possible. To make sure it gets the necessary attention, the compensation program is quickly redesigned with a value-management emphasis, and targets are given to managers to deliver value for the company in the next quarter.

This implementation suffers from numerous problems, including a lack of understanding and buy-in by people in the organization. Not taking the time to lay the foundation for implementation runs the risk of derailing the value-management program because the program is perceived as threatening to the status quo. When you use compensation to turbocharge the implementation, you must be very careful how you do it. Fooling around with people's pay without understanding the consequences is dynamite that can blow up the value program itself. In these cases, value management ends up as organizational road kill, run over by the unrealistic expectation for implementation and a lack of ownership by people in the company.

Trap 3: Measurement is King

A common reason for the failure to implement value-based management into an organization lies in overfocusing on the measure itself. This problem originates with an honest desire to get the measure "right." Getting the measure right is an important part of a successful implementation. However, no measure will ever be completely accurate, and it often makes sense to use different measures of value in different cases. For instance, you might use one measure of value for planning purposes and a simpler one for management reporting on existing operations.

An example is the company where it is so important to get the number right to a certain decimal point that management will spend years fine-tuning the calculation before proceeding with implementation. An example of this desire for accuracy is a leasing company that was so focused on getting the numbers right they spent two years on the measure to get it to where they felt comfortable. In those two years, the business was deteriorating so rapidly that the company was sold, and value-management became a moot point.

It makes sense to have a measure that accurately represents the underlying business economics, and it makes sense to spend the time to get the numbers right; however, value management is about improving decision making, not about counting pennies. Companies with highly analytical staffs run the risk of not seeing the forest for the trees by allowing the measure to overwhelm the implementation. In cases like this, the implementation will die of its own weight, and the company will have little to show for the effort.

Value management is a way to make decisions focused on creating value. It incorporates many factors, such as a measurement technique, analytic expertise, and calculations. None of these things in and of themselves are value management. The most common mistake is to assume the measure of value is management of value. Think of the measure as a translator that can take the information you give it on sales, cost, investment, and so on and translate it into value that you can compare with today's or yesterday's to determine how much value was or will be created. The measure itself does not create value; it just measures value.

Value management is not a replacement for good operational decision making. Value management is not a black box. There are measurements that require a computer to calculate value. Calculating value is necessary but not sufficient. Using a black box may be desirable in some instances to increase the accuracy of the calculation; however, in and of itself the black box has no value. The value of the measure stems from the ability of the management team to make decisions that create value from the information provided by the measure, regardless of whether the measure is calculated using a black box, a calculator, or a pencil and paper. Increased accuracy in and of itself without use in decision making has no value and wastes tremendous amounts of time.

Value management is not a crystal ball. It is not a replacement for management judgment. The measure itself is only as good as the information it is based on. The measure has no knowledge of the future and cannot predict what will happen. The measure knows nothing of business intentions, marginal effects, people, capabilities, and so on. The measure will not tell you how much your customers will buy from you next quarter or what your operating costs will be. The reverse is what really happens because you need to provide information on future sales and costs, and the value measure can then translate the information you give it into a measure of the value created.

Trap 4: Analysis Paralysis

Complexity is a common reason why value management goes off track and implementation fails. Different groups in the company have different agendas. In cases where the value-management program is brought in by the staff organization, there is the risk of the value-management program withering from analysis paralysis. This occurs because staff is too concerned about perfecting the measure and analyzing potential consequences and not concerned enough about demonstrating the real value of the program. This is the opposite of Trap 1 but just as deadly a menace to the program.

For a value-management implementation program to be successful, the operating managers have to adopt it. Operating managers will not adopt it if they do not understand it or if it is too complex to be used. The measure itself is the prime driver of complexity, and the complexity can and should be controlled. Although it is desirable to have a measure be as analytically robust as possible, the measure has to be simple enough to be used. This is a delicate balancing act and one that must be addressed for implementation to succeed.

One large consumer goods company was very interested in getting the "right" measure. They spent over two years in staff analysis before taking the measure to the operating groups. Could this analysis of the right measure have been done faster? You bet!

Trap 5: Everyone Speaks Finance

Line managers think in terms of their operating results, not in terms of finance or value creation. This difference in the way operating managers and financial managers think leads to misunderstanding. *Value management* is a foreign term to most line managers. Not everyone speaks finance or has a Ph.D. in finance and accounting. Companies that fall into this trap either assume that everyone does speak finance or try to train a large group of managers in finance and accounting. The response to this problem is the opposite: Translate value management and its terminology into the language of the operating manager. This will help achieve a higher level of understanding rather than trying to make the operating manager into a financial manager.

Occasionally, a company will fall into the trap of trying to make the measure all things to all people. This approach will doom the value effort to failure. No measure can account for all the possible circumstances in a complex business without being hideously complex, and the complexity will kill the effort.

One example of this is a multinational food and beverage company that decided to use economic value added as the value measure for the entire organization. The CEO became such a convert to value and the measurement that he insisted on measuring it in real time. The measure does not work in real time because the assets do not change that rapidly, and the operating management was less than enthusiastic about a daily measurement of how much value they were adding. The implementation stalled largely because the measurement became more important than the decisions it was supporting. The allure of using a single measure is strong, and management can find the simplicity of a single measure attractive. However, a single measure will not likely capture all the characteristics of the business, and use of a single measure is fraught with peril because it can drive poor decision making. Understanding the trade-off between profit and growth is normally very important.

HOW TO AVOID THE TRAPS

A little good planning can go a long way in avoiding these five traps. Start by making a compelling case to management for value and getting the commitment to the program with realistic expectations for time frame and implementation sequencing. Build a plan for adoption that focuses on achieving understanding and buy-in, and structure an implementation plan as described in Chapter 9.

Management avoids examining the trade-offs involved in managing for value at its own risk. Managing for value is a straightforward process that if used correctly can contribute value to the company and employees, and can help management build competitive advantage. The result for the owners is increased value.

CHAPTER 11

Summary

Investors require a return for their investment. The role of management is to deliver the required return to investors while balancing the interests of other stakeholders and ensuring the long-term viability of the business. This is a tall order, but with the objective of creating value for investors in mind, management develops strategies that describe how management will operate the business to deliver the return that investors require.

Management cannot stop at strategy but must continue by translating the strategy into tangible results for the investors. Strategies are the plan, but to paraphrase Knute Rockne, the real value is in the execution. Management needs tools to help them execute their strategies. One of the most powerful tools at management's disposal is performance measurement. Performance measures, when used correctly and aligned across management processes, send a powerful, consistent message of value creation to managers and encourage good decision making.

Value is created in the operating and investment decisions that managers make on a daily basis. For value management to succeed, it has to be embedded into the company's decision-making mind-set. This means attaining a high level of managerial understanding about how management can and does influence the value the company creates. Here, the critical step involves translating the abstract concept of value creation into meaningful day-to-day operating terms through the use of operating value drivers.

Value management is a mind-set. This mind-set has to be implemented into the company. Implementation is rarely easy or straightforward. Numerous pitfalls and common errors can derail the best of plans.

Value management is an important issue for many companies that are faced with pressure from investors or with the need to compete more effectively. Getting started can be a substantial roadblock to success because senior management looks at the enormity of the task and concludes that the scope is too great. This is unfortunate because although value management takes awhile to become fully embedded in a company, getting started is easy and straightforward. The important thing is not so much *where* you begin but *that* you begin.

The journey is worth the reward, as our friends at Acme (discussed in Chapter 1) discovered. They used value management as a tool to enforce management discipline and delivered superior returns to their shareholders as a result. Many companies are seeking to understand how to create value in the post-reengineering business world where value creation involves managing the delicate balance between profitability and growth. Each company and situation is different. The dynamics of the management team as well as their capabilities will dictate the form value management should take; there is no such thing as an effective off-the-shelf value-management solution. The off-the-shelf versions such as the packaged EVA® programs are too simplistic and fail to account for the underlying business issues the company is facing. These programs do not explain how the underlying business issues will influence the decisions managers make and the value they create.

Here are a few tips for getting started with a value-management program that will work for your company:

- Strive to create understanding first.
- Do not lead with compensation—unless you understand the risks.
- Focus on strategy and business issues—not the measures.
- Plan on a two- to three-year process for value-management implementation.
- Focus on facts, not opinions.
- Build early successes.
- Recognize that the information does not have to be perfect for you to begin.
- Customize the measure; do not use off-the-shelf solutions because every company is different.
- Review your key management processes to determine the alignment of the signals they are sending.
- Plan on including incentive compensation in your program.
- Remember that value management is a change process, and the process has to be managed to be effective.

Value management is a powerful tool. When used correctly to focus managers, it will drive dramatic improvements in decision making. However, like any other tool, it can be misused. Take the time to understand what objectives you are trying to achieve and how your business issues should drive a customized approach to value management. Then take the time to customize the measures you use and the way they are integrated into the company. The time and effort required to make value management a success will be worth the investment.

Endnotes

CHAPTER 1

1. There are exceptions where the company's mission is something other than maximizing value for the owners. Examples include nonprofit companies and for-profit companies where the largest shareholder(s) has different goals, such as Occidental Petroleum under Armand Hammer and the ownership of a large block of Kellogg stock by the Kellogg foundation.

CHAPTER 2

1. IBM had 547.8 million shares outstanding on 1-1-96 and 515.0 million shares outstanding on 12-31-96.

CHAPTER 3

1. Michael Hammer, *Beyond Reengineering, How the 21st Century Corporation is Reshaping* (New York: Harper Collins, 1996).
2. Berkshire Hathaway Annual Report, 1996.

3. "Destroying the Myths Surrounding Shareholder Value,"
SCA Consulting, May 1996.

CHAPTER 5

1. Love Field flights were limited by federal law as specified in
the Wright Amendment.

CHAPTER 6

1. In Illinois, for many years the state banking laws permitted
banks only one location. The local-market emphasis in
banking can be traced in part back to the William Jennings
Bryan populist politics of the turn of the last century and
the average person's distrust of large financial institutions.
2. LIBOR: London/Interbank rate.
3. Moore's law states that the number of transistors on a chip
will double every 18 months.
4. Economies of scale and the effects of the experience curve
are discussed in the Boston Consulting Group, *Perspectives
on Experience*, 1972.

CHAPTER 7

1. As of February 1997, based on five years of earnings.
2. Benjamin Graham, David L. Dodd, Sidney Cottle, *Security
Analysis, Principals and Technique*, 4th ed (New York:
McGraw-Hill, 1962), p. 477.
3. Gregory Millman, "Taking the Lies out of Earnings," *Worth*,
February, 1997.
4. *Summa de Arithmetica.*
5. EVA and MVA are registered trademarks of Stern Stewart &
Co. Because Stern Stewart has chosen to trademark the
letters EVA, many companies are using other terms, such as
economic profit (EP), shareholder value added (SVA), or
cash value added (CVA) for the same concept.

6. Spot Value is the net present value of the future cash flow to equity holders.

7. Plan value is the value of the actual cash flows during the planning period plus the spot value of the end of the plan.

8. DCFS is a technique used to simulate future cash flows, including a fade and growth assumption.

9. Robert S. Koplar and David P. Norton, *The Balanced Scorecard* (Harvard Business School Press, 1996).

CHAPTER 8

1. I recommend reading the following for a complete treatment of this subject: Bruce R. Ellig, *Executive Compensation—A Total Perspective* (New York: McGraw-Hill, 1982) and Robert E. Sibson, *Compensation*, AMA Conference, New York, 1990.

James A. Knight is the managing partner of SCA Consulting's Value Management and Performance Measurement Practice. SCA, an international management consulting firm, combines its strategy, finance, and compensation expertise to assist leading companies in establishing and achieving effective strategies. Knight was formerly a leader of The Boston Consulting Group's Value Management Practice.

Contact Information:
www.scaconsulting.com
jknight@chi.scaconsulting.com